American Antiques ❧ 1800-1900

American Antiques 1800-1900

A Collector's History and Guide

BY JOSEPH T. BUTLER

THE ODYSSEY PRESS · NEW YORK

Preface

THIS BOOK is intended for collectors who are anxious to explore an area that has still not been completely charted. It is hoped that the reader will glean some historical background on the objects discussed as well as some hints on present-day collecting possibilities. Only the most basic technical information on the manufacture of the various objects is included.

All of the plates in the book show objects that were made in the United States. In as many instances as possible, the objects chosen are being shown here for the first time. It was necessary, however, to include certain "classics" which might be old friends of the reader. Where it has seemed feasible, figures drawn from nineteenth century printed sources have been included. While most of these figures have been taken from American publications, some come from English sources known to have been used by craftsmen in the United States.

Only the decorative arts have been included, and there are, of course, certain omissions in this area. It has been the author's task to decide which subjects would be most interesting to the twentieth century collector. The sources noted in the bibliography will guide the reader to further information.

The emphasis is placed on high-style objects rather than those of country make. Country furnishings are best understood in the light of their relationship to a more sophisticated formal style.

It is hoped that this work will interest others to investigate further America's decorative arts originating between 1800 and 1900.

Dobbs Ferry, New York   J. T. B.

Acknowledgments

A NUMBER of friends and colleagues have given generously of their time and energy to be of assistance in the preparation of this book. They have helped in locating photographs and providing critical comments on sections of the text. Special thanks are due to James Biddle and Berry B. Tracy, the Metropolitan Museum of Art; George O. Bird and Gerald G. Gibson, Henry Ford Museum; Charles Brownell, Birmingham, Michigan; Frank L. DuMond, Grand Rapids Public Museum; Benjamin Ginsburg, New York City; Richard H. Howland and Miss Rodris Roth, Smithsonian Institution; Mrs. Harold Kraft, Sagamore Hill; Miss Elinor Merrell, New York City; Milo Naeve and John A. H. Sweeney, The Henry Francis du Pont Winterthur Museum; Mrs. Celia Jackson Otto, Mt. Vernon, New York; Miss Patricia E. Smith, Sleepy Hollow Restorations; Richard Randall, The Walters Art Gallery; Paula D. Sampson, Old Sturbridge Village; Marvin D. Schwartz, The Brooklyn Museum; Dr. Robert C. Smith, University of Pennsylvania; Miss Margaret Stearns, Museum of the City of New York; and Miss Alice Winchester, *Antiques*.

While credit of ownership is indicated with each photograph which is shown, the private collectors who have allowed me to include objects must be warmly thanked. They are Mr. and Mrs. Charles J. Biddle, Mr. and Mrs. James Biddle, Mr. and Mrs. Carl Carmer, Mrs. Stephen C. Clark, Mr. and Mrs. John deMenil, Mrs. Singleton Gardner, Mrs. Benjamin Ginsburg, Princess Artchil Gourielli, Miss Natalie Hays Hammond, William Hill, Edgar J. Kaufmann, jr., Mr. and Mrs. John H. Kerr, Mr. and Mrs. George W. Marshall, Henry P. McIlhenny, Mrs. Lydia Bond Powel, Miss Caroline Rutter, and Mrs. Giles Whiting.

Photographic Credits: The following individuals and institutions are acknowledged as having provided or taken photographs used in this book:

Antiques, Ill. 22; Gilbert Ask, Ills. D, 12, 15, 18, 81, 88, 112; James Biddle, Ills. 7, 9; The Brooklyn Museum, Ills. 19, 31, 38, 41, 44, 54, 59, 61, 62, 65, 67, 68, 69, 70, 71, 72, 75, 76, 77, 78, 79, 80, 104, 113, 114, 115, 116; John L. DiLillo, Ill. 50; Henry Ford Museum, Ills. 30, 45, 46, 47, 51, 52, 53, 55, 56, 57, 58, 60, 63, 64, 73, 74, 89, 90, 91, 92, 93; Louis Frohman, Ill. 66; Ginsburg and Levy, Inc., Ills. 2, 5; Clarence Laughlin, Ills. 123, 124; The Metropolitan Museum, Ill. 11; Mr. and Mrs. George Montgomery, Ill. 33; Museum of the City of New York, Ills. 20, 24, 105, 106, 111; Museum of Fine Arts, Boston, Ills. 1, 14, 43; The Newark Museum, Ills. 23, 40; Philadelphia Museum of Art, Ill. 3; Thurman Rotan, Ills. F, G, H, 4, 6, 10, 13, 16, 17, 21, 25, 26, 27, 28, 32, 34, 35, 36, 37, 39, 42, 45, 48, 49, 82, 83, 84, 85, 86, 87, 94, 95, 96, 97, 98, 99, 100, 101, 102, 103, 107, 108, 109, 110, 117, 118, 119, 120, 121, 122, and all Figures; Sleepy Hollow Restorations, Ill. B and C; Robert C. Smith, Ill. A; Smithsonian Institution, Ill. 29; Taylor and Dull, Ill. 8; Donald Sultner Wells, Ill. E.

Contents

Illustrations

ILLUSTRATIONS

ILLUSTRATIONS

ILLUSTRATIONS

xvi

ILLUSTRATIONS

FIGURES

ILLUSTRATIONS

American Antiques ❦ 1800-1900

Some Notes about the United States in the Nineteenth Century

THE DECORATIVE ARTS of any period are best understood within the overall historical context of the age in which they were produced. This is especially true of the nineteenth century arts, because in no previous historical period was there such rapid and constant change in all the institutions of society. Indeed, progress is probably the key word in any such discussion, for man during the nineteenth century held this goal above all others.

The birth of Queen Victoria in 1819 was virtually coincident with the beginnings of the industrial age in England and the United States. Some experimentation had been done with power machinery during the late eighteenth century, but it was not until the early nineteenth century that steam began to be harnessed successfully for a wide range of tasks. After the War of 1812, manufacturing replaced earlier commercial interests, especially in New England, and the abundance of skilled labor and water power guaranteed success to the factory system. The Industrial Revolution meant that more products were now available to the nation because of mass production. It was also responsible for the development, by the middle of the century, of synthetics and new metallic alloys.

Another important outgrowth of the Industrial Revolution came in the field of transportation. The great strides made here opened entire new areas for exploitation and development. By the late 1820's the first railroads were being constructed in the United States. Indeed, the railroad and steamship, by linking not only previously isolated parts of countries but separate continents as well, were responsible for the change of entire centers of manufacture; they effectively reduced distances to as little as one eighth of their previous spans.

The greatest strides in railroad transportation occurred during the second half of the century; in 1865 there were thirty-five thousand miles of track in the United States, while by 1900 this mileage had increased to nearly two hundred thousand. Each additional mile of track brought greater financial opportunities to both the industrialist and the merchant because goods could now be conveyed longer distances at lower cost. Progress in transportation also gave a backbone to migrations of settlers to previously unexplored or unsettled western lands. Linked with transportation was communication. Steamships and the postal service caused contact between nations and continents to be more rapid. With the invention of the telegraph and, later in the century, the laying of the Atlantic Cable and the development of the telephone, an important event in any country could have immediate world-wide impact.

The machine also brought about a complete breakdown in the guild or apprentice system of craftsmanship. Now mechanized equipment could do the work of the individual craftsman, so the traditional significance of handwork vanished. A single object, instead of being the visualization and creation of an individual, became the mass-produced result of the efforts of any number of workers.

Mechanization was also responsible for opening and developing vast new markets for inexpensive products. A completely new division of responsibility developed between the manufacturer and distributor. In the eighteenth century it was quite common for the craftsman to market his own product; in the nineteenth century he turned it over to a retail distributor, thus laying the foundations for the marketing system which has existed ever since. Increased mechanization also eliminated numbers of jobs that previously had been done by hand—thereby creating a major problem of unemployment. A new type of occupation came into being, however, because trained mechanics were now necessary to tend the machines.

Agriculture also underwent a revolution. Subsistence farming began to be replaced by the cash crop method. New machines such as the cotton gin, reaper, thresher, and binder, coupled with the development of new insecticides and fertilizers, greatly increased the yield of the land. At the same time the need for agricultural labor decreased and there was a heavy migration of people from the farm to the city.

The rapid growth of cities was one of the most conspicuous changes of the century. The migration from rural areas, coupled with the great immigration from abroad, caused the urban population of the United States to rise from one sixth of the total in 1860 to one third by 1900. Between 1880 and 1900 the number of American cities with a population of at least one hundred thousand increased from nineteen to thirty-six.

The nineteenth century saw a radical breakdown of the stratification of society. The middle class began to rise to much greater power. Shrewd investments in power industries and modern forms of transportation brought increased amounts of money into the grasp of this group. There were successive reforms throughout the century which bettered the lot of the working class and provided them with improved living conditions and more opportunities for education. In the second half of the century the working class became so strong that unions began to be organized and eventually were recognized by employers; the movement gained considerable strength in 1886 when the American Federation of Labor was organized.

The philosophical idea that everyone in a society is entitled to an education gained its strongest support in the United States. Indeed, the rapid acceleration of popular education was one of the dominant trends of the nineteenth century. During the eighteenth century, education was generally limited to the rich and was conducted on a lower level by private tutors; the student who had completed the necessary requirements was then admitted to a college or university. Mechanization was indirectly responsible for the trend toward popular education because power-driven printing presses could now turn out books in great quantities and improved transportation made them available in remote areas.

The study and teaching of the natural sciences also gained great momentum during the century. By 1847 the Harvard Astronomical Observatory was equipped with the world's largest telescope and in the following year the American Association for the Advancement of Science was organized in Boston. The publication of Charles Darwin's *Origin of Species* in 1859 presented a revolutionary concept of the evolution of man. During the second half of the century chemistry, geology, botany, and other basic sciences became standard courses in the college curriculum.

Nations began to vie with one another in creating elaborate products with their power-driven machines. It seemed that the more elaborate an object was, the more it demonstrated the skill of its designer and manufacturer. This competitive spirit was shown in the Great Exhibition of the Industry of All Nations which was held in London in 1851. It was to house this exhibition that Joseph Paxton designed his Crystal Palace. The building was greatly influenced by mechanized processes, for it was constructed of glass and iron girths with interchangeable parts—the whole resembling an enormous greenhouse. Nations from all over the world sent their best products to this exhibition. Science and industry played a dominant role in the individual displays and even the arts and crafts products showed the strong influence of mechanization. The displays revealed that science and engineering had now enveloped craftsmanship and that individual products were often of poor quality. Newspapers and commentators of the period focused full attention on the marvels of mechanization. Individual objects were often bulky in their overall line and were covered with flat pattern and applied ornament. Decorative motifs were borrowed from numerous historical sources; these were used in indiscriminate combinations with no real sense of original purpose.

The practice of holding international exhibitions was continued throughout the remainder of the century—typical were the London International Exhibition of 1862, the Philadelphia Centennial Exhibition of 1876, and the World's Columbian Exposition of 1892—and scientific progress was always the dominating theme of the displays. The decorative arts sections were dominated by over-elaborate objects that often were made completely or in part by machine. Ornament borrowed from historical sources was to be seen in the design of every kind of object, whether it was a machine decorated with Gothic tracery or a large sofa embellished with all the trappings of a Bourbon court.

The great mass of documentary material and objects that survive from the nineteenth century is often confusing and overwhelming to the present-day student. In the following chapters, which deal with various categories of the nineteenth century decorative arts, it might be well to bear in mind that the key to the period is change. Progress was as important in shaping the taste shown in the domestic interior as it was in forming the intellectual, economic, and social currents of the world in general.

1 Desk made of mahogany and satinwood, attributed to John Seymour of Boston, c. 1800. The tambour doors at the top close over a series of pigeonholes which are painted the characteristic blue-green of Seymour's work.

Museum of Fine Arts, Boston.

2 One of a pair of side chairs made of mahogany attributed to Duncan Phyfe, New York City, c. 1815. The curule, or Roman base with delicate paw feet, is well shown in these chairs.

Ginsburg & Levy, Inc.

3 Card table made of mahogany, attributed to Henry Connelly of Philadelphia, c. 1810. The "oak-leaf" type of acanthus carving seen on the leg was used by both Connelly and another Philadelphian, Ephraim Haines; each designed the foot in a highly individual manner.

Henry P. McIlhenny.

4 Side chair made of mahogany, attributed to Duncan Phyfe, New York City, c. 1815. This chair from a set of eight is a part of the wedding furniture made for Sophia Miles Belden; the double eagle head is an unusual detail.

Mrs. Giles Whiting.

FURNITURE

THE DESIGN and style of nineteenth century furniture were influenced by three dominant factors. The first of these was historical revivalism—the borrowing of decorative details, or indeed the entire design vocabulary, of a style which had been popular in the past. At times the overall effect of a piece of revival furniture was that of a reproduction of a model from the past; at other times antique elements were applied to a form of a completely different style. Historical revivalism survived in one manner or another throughout the entire century.

Around the middle of the century, and continuing until its end, there were certain designers and tastemakers who advocated a break with revivalism. These men were responsible for the second factor which must be considered—progressive tendencies in furniture design. The furniture produced under this influence was sometimes free from revival decoration, and in other instances it had some mechanical or technical innovation incorporated into it. The third influence on nineteenth century furniture was the utilization of new materials in design and construction. Although earlier furniture makers had occasionally used materials other than wood, the nineteenth century saw an increase in the use of such materials as iron, wire, tubular metal, papier-mâché, and different organic substances (cane, rattan, animal horn, etc.). However, historical revivalism, in its various aspects, was the predominant influence during the century.

European Background of the Classical Style. The first revival style which became important at the beginning of the nineteenth

31

century was the Classical. This was a style based on decorative motifs and actual furniture forms of ancient Greece and Rome. Since the furniture of nineteenth century America was still greatly influenced by taste in England and France, it might be well to summarize movements in these countries which were important in developing the Classical style.

As early as 1730 the English architect William Kent had begun to apply such Classical devices as Greek keys and egg-and-dart moldings to Baroque furniture. The furniture form did not change in any way, since Kent's innovation was merely application of alien devices to the surface of the piece. This step, which was the first in the creation of the Classical style, was copied by other designers in both England and France until the 1750's and 1760's. The second step was the development of a straight leg which was carved or turned, in contrast to the curvilinear lines of the popular Rococo style. Another English architect, Robert Adam, has sometimes been given credit for developing this innovation about 1765, but there is some evidence that the straight leg was also in use in France at about that time. Adam's ideas were translated into furniture designs by George Hepplewhite in his *Cabinet-Maker and Upholsterer's Guide* (1788) and Thomas Sheraton in his *The Cabinet-Maker and Upholsterer's Drawing-Book* (1791-1794). These books were a dominant influence in disseminating this phase of the Classical style. The third development in the creation of the Classical style was the copying of actual Greco-Roman furniture forms. The two forms most often copied were a chair form called *klismos* (see Ill. 4) and a bench and chair form called *curule* (see Ill. 2). The klismos form is composed of a horizontal solid cresting piece that supports the back with the front and rear legs, flaring outward in a saber line. The curule is the familiar X-shaped support that meets with the top of the bench and supports it on the floor.

32

These archaeological forms were used by two French designers, Charles Percier and Pierre F. L. Fontaine, who in 1801 (second edition 1812) published a collection of plates in this style which they called *Recueil de Décorations Intérieures.* ... These men were chiefly responsible for formulating what is called the Empire Style; when Napoleon Bonaparte established his Empire in 1804, he made Percier and Fontaine his official court decorators. Some of the Greco-Roman motifs that appeared in their work were acanthus leaves, cornucopias, swans, eagles, dolphins, and monopodia (combination of animal head and leg into a single element). The furniture and rooms shown in the *Recueil* were intended only for the wealthiest patrons. The furniture was made of mahogany and rosewood and elaborately decorated with ormolu mounts; it was massive and cubical in character. Napoleon's campaign in Egypt made popular another set of ancient decorative motifs that were incorporated into the Empire style. The massive solidity of Egyptian design was reflected in many furniture forms, and such motifs as the lotus, sphinx, hawk, and hieroglyphics were used as decorative detail.

After the Bourbon Restoration (1814-1830) the spirit of the Empire was still kept alive in cabinetmaking. The heaviness continued, although some of the Restoration and Charles X furniture was stripped of much of its ormolu detail. Fruitwoods (apple, orange, lemon) began to replace mahogany as favorites. The gondola chair, a modification of the klismos type in which the back was closed in, was popular in the Restoration and Louis Philippe (1830-1848) periods.

In England, Thomas Hope, a friend of Percier, published an important book on furniture design early in the nineteenth century —*Household Furniture and Interior Decoration* (1807). Hope was a wealthy amateur who had traveled extensively in the Mediterranean area collecting classical antiques. His book contained designs for his London house as well as for a country residence and the furniture was designed so that it would be harmonious with his collections. He used the same design vocabulary as Percier and Fontaine; the klismos and curule forms remain dominant. It was Hope's designs that were instrumental in creating what is generally called the English Regency style. His was not, however, the first book of English Regency designs to be published, for a later edition of Thomas Sheraton's *The Cabinet-Maker and Upholsterer's Drawing Book* (1802) contained furniture in the same style. This work, along with his *Designs for Household Furniture* (published after his death in 1812), shows a distinct break with the tradition of Adamesque Classicism in which he and Hepplewhite had long worked.

Hope's designs were intended, as were those of Percier and Fontaine, for the wealthy. Almost simultaneously with the appearance of *Household Furniture,* there was a strong movement toward coarsening this furniture for popular consumption. Furniture became more massive and a heavy bulbousness began to appear in supports. Architectural scrolled pediments, heavy columns with capitals in all the Classical orders, and winged lion's-paw feet began to appear in furniture design. One of the chief proponents and disseminators of this debased style was George Smith. He published a work called *A Collection of Designs for Household Furniture and Interior Decoration* in 1808. Smith's work is characterized by a lack of the archaeological exactness of Hope and his French contemporaries. In a second work, *The Cabinet Maker and Upholsterer's Guide* (1826), the same coarsening, heaviness, and massive solidity are to be observed. The changes in popular furniture design can also be observed in a monthly periodical, Rudolph Ackermann's *Repository of Arts, Literature, Fashions, etc.,* which appeared between 1809 and 1829. John Claudius Loudon published the first edition (of many to follow) of his *Encyclopaedia of Cottage, Farm and Villa Architecture and Furniture* in 1833. This was a work which greatly popularized furniture design and brought new furniture designs within the reach of the average working man. Each of these works advocated similar furniture forms. Chief among these was the loo table (named after a popular game) which had a round or square top and heavy turned pedestal which terminated in massive claw feet. Sofas were straight, massive and decorated with exaggerated cornucopias and winged lion's-claw feet. Chairs retained the klismos shape but the front legs were often straight with reeded and turned detail rather than in the saber curve.

Another element that was important in influencing English Regency furniture was the cult of the picturesque—the introduction of many bizarre and fanciful motifs, often derived from Hindu and Chinese sources, into furniture design. This taste was popular at the same time as the Classical style. Certainly the most elaborate result of this taste was the Brighton Pavilion which was built for the Prince of Wales in 1815 by John Nash and decorated by Frederick Crace.

Thus, the development of the Classical style has been traced from its beginning with application of Greco-Roman motifs to Baroque furniture forms, to the development of the round tapering leg and Classical-inspired furniture, through the archaeological interpretation, and finally the coarsening and debasing of the Classical style. Now it is time to see how this style influenced the furniture of the new republic.

Classicism in the United States, 1800-1850. The European Classical style first influenced furniture design in America about 1780. The first phase was that of the inspiration of Classical devices. Furniture produced in this taste was based on the design books of Hepplewhite and Sheraton, and the light straight leg and shield back were distinguishing details. This style of furniture is generally referred to as Federal, and notable examples were made in several centers along the Eastern seaboard. Such important cabinetmakers as Samuel McIntire and William Hook of Salem, Thomas and John Seymour of Boston, and Ephraim Haines and Henry Connelly of Philadelphia all executed masterworks in this style (see Ills. 1 & 3). The Empire style, which was the second step in the development of the American Classical style, became popular in the early years of the nineteenth century (c. 1810) and continued to be in vogue until about 1825. It was after this that the heavy and debased style became popular and remained in fashion as late as 1850.

The Empire style was transmitted first to New York while the other cities important for cabinetmaking continued to produce furniture in the Federal style. Certainly the most important individual in setting the Empire style was the cabinetmaker Duncan Phyfe (1768-1854). Phyfe migrated from Scotland to America about 1783. He settled briefly in Albany and then moved on to New York where he was first listed in the *Directory* in 1792. He moved to Partition Street in 1795 and maintained the city's most fashionable cabinetmaking shop. His style evolved from the Federal through the Empire and into an early and traditional version of the Louis XV revival style, for he did not retire until 1847. His designs have such an individual interpretation of elements from the English Regency that it might be said that Phyfe created his own style. He must have been familiar with the Regency designs of Sheraton's *Cabinet Dictionary*, for he was using saber legs on klismos chairs as early as 1807 (see Ill. 4). Other forms which Phyfe made popular were the curule, or Roman base, on chairs and settees (see Ill. 2), chairs with a lyre splat, the Grecian or Récamier couch with scrolled ends, and cabinet pieces with the Egyptian animal leg and foot. The latest of Phyfe's productions, such as his

Voltaire chairs, show the beginnings of the reintroduction of curved line into furniture design.

Another cabinetmaker who was important in setting the Empire style in New York was Charles-Honoré Lannuier (1779-1819). He migrated to New York from France in 1803, and his work shows the influence of both the French Directoire and Empire styles. Lannuier's furniture is often more ornate than that of Phyfe and was characteristically decorated with elaborate ormolu mounts. His excellence as a cabinetmaker is seen in the sculpturesque quality of the carved figures which he incorporated into furniture (see Ill. 5).

There were many other master cabinetmakers on the Eastern seaboard who produced Classical-inspired furniture (see Ill. 6). Sometimes extremely interesting examples were produced of native woods, maple being chief among these (see Ills. 7 & 9). In several rare instances Grecian furniture forms were duplicated with remarkable archaeological exactness in American furniture (see Ill. 8). An extremely curious armchair in the Classical style survives at the First Unitarian Church in Baltimore, Maryland; it is attributed to the building's architect Maximilian Godefroy (fl. 1806-1824) (see Color Plate A). Because European design publications were reaching America more quickly than they had previously, the influence of Smith's *Guide* was felt here as early as 1830. The column with ornate capital began to appear on cabinet furniture at this time (see Ill. 10) and the winged lion's-paw foot was frequently seen on sofas (see Ill. 11). Stenciled decoration was increasingly popular after 1815; it became one of the chief characteristics of high style furniture (see Ill. 12).

Allied with stenciling was the production of "fancy" chairs. These were Sheraton chairs of light construction, generally with rush or caned seats, and painted or japanned decoration. The cresting piece of such chairs was often painted with a romanticized

5 Sofa table made of mahogany highlighted with gilt, attributed to Charles-Honoré Lannuier, New York City, c. 1818. The sculpturesque carving of the eagle, a masterful handling of Empire decoration, causes this to be a significant example of the cabinetmaker's work.

Ginsburg & Levy, Inc.

6 Card table made of mahogany probably in New York, c. 1815-1825. The use of the lyre with swan-head terminations and the basket of flowers is unusual in such a combination.

Author's collection.

scene; sometimes the backs were actually shaped into a full motif of an eagle, shield, or other patriotic emblem (see Ill. 13). A remarkable set of chairs closely connected with the "fancy" Sheraton type was made about 1815 by a Boston cabinetmaker, S. Gragg. They were made of oak and hickory painted a solid color and then decorated with peacock feathers. Probably intended for garden use, they are an unusual American variant of the klismos type (see Ill. 14). Probably the best known type of "fancy" chair produced in America at the time was made by Lambert Hitchcock at his factory at Hitchcocksville, Connecticut. These were mass produced, had stencil decoration and were popular in many parts of America (see Ill. 18). A religious sect, the Shakers, also began to produce a unique type of furniture in the early nineteenth century. They originally settled in New York State but migrated to other places and produced a type of furniture of profound simplicity in a modified Classical style (see Ill. 15).

During the 1830's an even greater massiveness began to dominate furniture design, and plain, undecorated surfaces and scroll supports began to appear, distinctly influenced by the design of the French Restoration period. One of the most important cabinet-making firms in the dissemination of this last phase of Classicism in America was Joseph Meeks and Sons (1797-1868) of New York. In 1833, Endicott & Semett printed a colored lithograph for the firm which showed 41 pieces of furniture and two sets of draperies. This print is of great importance for it is the first American publication which illustrates complete furniture designs (Fig. 1). The furniture was in the style which was most popular at the time—the late Classical. The pieces of cabinet furniture shown in the print have projecting columns in the French manner and there is an extraordinary use of S and C scrolls in all forms. Indeed, it might be said that the scroll is the key to the style of the 1830's (see Ill. 17). The French bed (bed with scrolled head and foot

Fig. 1 Broadside of Joseph Meeks & Sons (1797-1868) printed by Endicott & Semett in New York City in 1833. The complete vocabulary of the American late Classical style is shown in this broadside; pier tables, center tables and sideboards demonstrate the massive quality of this style.

board the same height) continued to be popular although they were now generally stripped of Classical ornament (see Ill. 16). A bed of this type, with elaborate drapery, was shown in the Meeks advertisement. Because of the striking shape, the term "sleigh bed" has been attached generally to this form.

The most popular medium through which the scroll or plain Classical style was circulated was a Baltimore publication of

7 Side chair made of maple, probably in Philadelphia, c. 1830. The cresting piece and central back support are treated in a highly original manner for the klismos form; from Nicholas Biddle's house, "Andalusia."

Mr. & Mrs. Charles J. Biddle.

8 Side chair made of mahogany veneer with ebony inlay, probably in New York, or Philadelphia, c. 1815-1825. This example is archaeologically correct in its interpretation of the klismos type.

Mrs. Lydia Bond Powel.

9 Sofa made of maple, probably in Philadelphia, c. 1830. The low back and flat relief carving make this sofa a superb example of the American Empire style; from Nicholas Biddle's house, "Andalusia."

Mr. & Mrs. Charles J. Biddle.

10 Sideboard made of mahogany veneer probably in New York, c. 1835. The use of the full free-standing Classical order with base and capital plus the lion monopodium is well demonstrated in this piece.

Sleepy Hollow Restorations. Gift of T. W. S. Phillips.

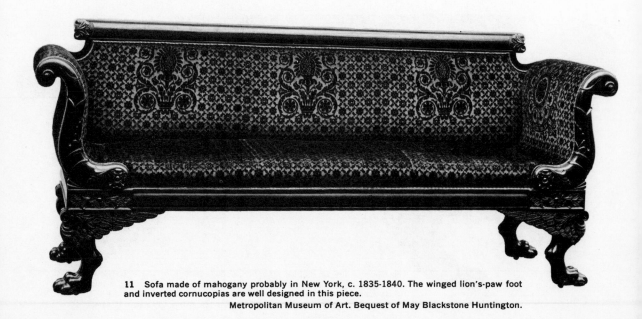

11 Sofa made of mahogany probably in New York, c. 1835-1840. The winged lion's-paw foot and inverted cornucopias are well designed in this piece.

Metropolitan Museum of Art. Bequest of May Blackstone Huntington.

Fig. 2 Plate from John Hall's *Cabinet Maker's Assistant*, published in Baltimore in 1840. The sofa and footstools incorporate the C and S scrolls which Hall advocated.

1840—John Hall's *The Cabinet Maker's Assistant*. This book contains 198 plates which show all furniture forms completely dominated in design by single and double scrolls. Hall believed that the elliptical curve was the most beautiful single ingredient of design. His furniture designs, intended for inexpensive pieces whose parts could be cut with a bandsaw, reduced carving to a minimum. The monotonous use of the scrolls is well observed in his designs for footstools (Figs. 2 and 3). They are inverted and

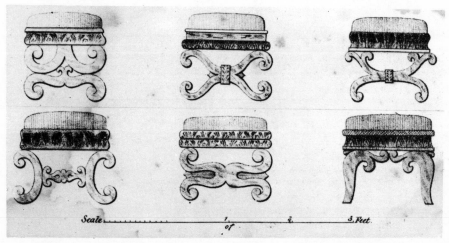

Fig. 3 Plate from Hall's *Cabinet Maker's Assistant* showing stools conceived of scrolls cut by a jigsaw.

43

changed about in every conceivable way although several still retain some similarity to the curule form; others are dominated by a simple flattened S scroll. It was only in large wardrobes and other pieces of cabinet furniture that Hall was not able to completely dominate the form of the piece with scrolls (Fig. 4).

One of the interesting factors about the Classical style is that it continued to be popular into the early 1850's. The purveyor of popular taste in England during the first half of the century was John C. Loudon. His *Encyclopaedia,* which was issued in numerous editions, was well known in the United States and had considerable influence. In an edition as late as 1853, Loudon showed a plate illustrating chairs of a modified klismos type (Fig. 5). In each of these examples the flaring front saber leg has disappeared and

Fig. 4 Wardrobes shown in Hall's *Cabinet Maker's Assistant* were ponderous and conceived in the debased versions of the late Classical style.

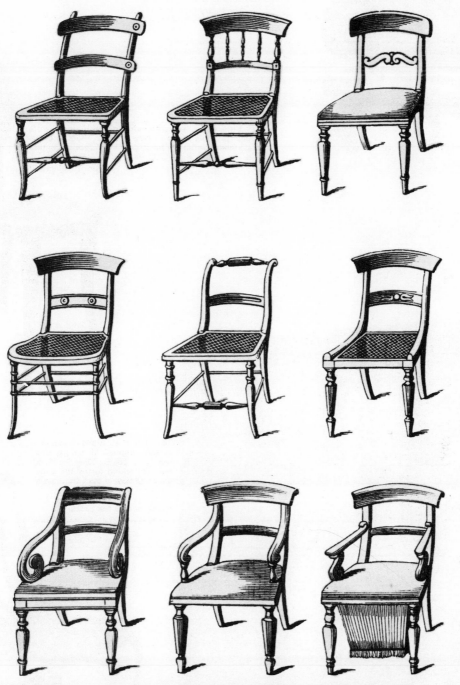

Fig. 5 Plate from J. C. Loudon's *Encyclopaedia of Cottage, Farm and Villa Architecture and Furniture*, published in London in 1853. All of the variations of the late Empire chair back, which were eventually interpreted in America, are shown in this plate.

45

12 Armchair with gilt and ebonized decoration, made in New York, c. 1840. The crispness of detail and intricacy of stenciled decoration make this chair a masterwork in the New York Empire style.

The Henry Francis du Pont Winterthur Museum.

13 Side chair, with polychrome paint over soft woods, possibly made in New York, c. 1835. The full eagle which forms the back, plus the Egyptian revival legs, make this a rarity in American furniture.

Author's collection.

14 Side chair made of ash and hickory, signed "S. Gragg, Boston," c. 1815. The S-shaped member which forms the back, seat and legs is bent from a single piece of wood, making this a prototype of the bentwood seen at the end of the century.

Museum of Fine Arts, Boston.

15 Room end made in the Shaker Community at Endfield, New Hampshire, c. 1840. A simplified version of Classical architectural detail is shown in this room end as in other forms of Shaker furniture.

The Henry Francis du Pont Winterthur Museum.

has been replaced with a turned leg. In the United States, Andrew Jackson Downing (1815-1852) was very much aware of Loudon's work and acknowledged the debt he owed to this source. Downing was highly influential in setting American taste during the middle of the century. In 1850, in his *Architecture of Country Houses,* Downing was still advocating the Classical or Grecian style, which he maintained was the most popular for private residences. He included a plate in this work which showed three chairs in a heavy version of the archaeologically Classical style (Fig. 6).

The Gothic Revival Style. The Gothic was another style which Downing favored and discussed in the furniture section of his *Architecture of Country Houses.* He said that this style was not as popular nor as well known in the United States as in Europe and that the general objection to furniture of this type was that it was too elaborate and was often made to resemble the front of a cathedral. Downing believed that furniture simply made in the Gothic style was quite suitable for hall or "ordinary room" use (Fig. 7). Indeed, the small amount of American Gothic furniture which survives testifies to its general lack of popularity.

Fig. 6 Three chairs from Andrew J. Downing's *Architecture of Country Houses,* published in New York in 1850. These chairs, which are surprisingly archeologically correct, were late examples of their type.

47

This style was very popular in England, where it had never completely died out from medieval times. As with the Classical style, the first phase of this revival was the mere application of Gothic devices to then contemporary furniture forms. This was done in the early eighteenth century by William Kent and continued later by Thomas Chippendale, who published furniture patterns with Gothic tracery in his *The Gentleman and Cabinet-Maker's Directory* of 1754. One of the chief enthusiasts of the style in England was Horace Walpole; his house, "Strawberry Hill," was Gothic both inside and out.

Gothic waned in popularity toward the end of the eighteenth century but again came to life in the early nineteenth century because of the popularity of the writings of the British romantics. Smith's *Household Furniture* of 1808, which showed much furniture in the Classical taste, also included designs in a careful and more exacting Gothic style. None of the pieces, however, archaeologically imitated actual medieval furniture forms.

In 1817 Ackermann's *Repository* first showed Gothic furniture; this same publication included Gothic designs by a writer on medieval architecture, Augustus Charles Pugin, which were col-

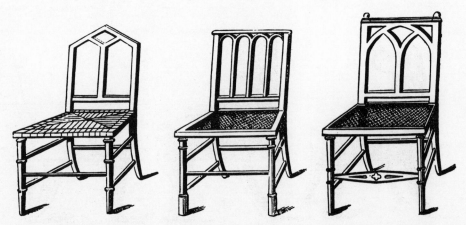

Fig. 7 Three chairs from Downing's *Country Houses* which are in the Gothic revival style. Each of these examples includes Gothic decorative detail combined in a highly individual manner.

16 Bed made of mahogany veneer and mahogany, c. 1840. The French or "Sleigh" bed was pushed against the wall and generally hung with a canopy which extended over both its ends.

Sleepy Hollow Restorations.

17 Card table made of mahogany veneer over light wood probably in New York, c. 1840. This American interpretation of the French Restoration style shows the elimination of excess Classical detail which typifies this style.

Mr. & Mrs. John H. Kerr.

19 Side chair made of mahogany, c. 1835. The pointed arches and trefoil are Gothic revival elements incorporated into the back of an otherwise Classical chair.

The Brooklyn Museum.

18 Side chair made of painted light wood bearing the stenciled label of Lambert Hitchcock of Hitchcocksville (Conn.), c. 1835. These chairs were mass produced and rank among the most popular made in early 19th century America.

The Henry Francis du Pont Winterthur Museum.

lected in book form in 1827. Pugin's son, Augustus W. N. Pugin, who worked with Sir Charles Barry in remodeling the Houses of Parliament, published his *Gothic Furniture in the Style of the Fifteenth Century* in 1835. The designs of both Pugins were extremely elaborate, intricate, and often impractical for execution. Henry Shaw's *Specimens of Ancient Furniture* (London, 1836) was the first book on English antique furniture. It contained several plates showing medieval pieces, and this helped give impetus to the movement.

The chief design motifs employed in Gothic furniture were the pointed and lancet arches, rosettes, heraldic devices, crockets, trefoils, finials, and tracery. Often one or more of these motifs might be incorporated into a piece that was essentially Classical in overall appearance (see Ill. 19). The first Gothic furniture in the United States probably appeared during the second quarter of the nineteenth century; this was furniture in the late Classical style which incorporated a few Gothic motifs. Much of the best American Gothic furniture was designed by architects, for the style was much more successfully handled architecturally. Chief among these was Alexander J. Davis, who designed highly sophisticated furniture and mirror frames to be used *en suite* with his interior woodwork (see Ill. 20). Indeed, when the architect Thomas U. Walter and Nicholas Biddle together designed the latter's house "Andalusia" on the banks of the Delaware River, the main house was in the Classical style while another small house on the property was built and furnished in the Gothic Style (see Ill. 22).

Robert Conner, a pupil of George Smith in England, migrated to New York and in 1842 published his *Cabinet Maker's Assistant* there; this was the first design book of Gothic furniture to be published in the United States. In the New York area Gothic furniture was made by Richard Byrnes of White Plains and John Jelliff of Newark, New Jersey. The surviving designs of

Byrnes reveal that he handled the incorporation of Gothic motifs into the overall effect of the piece in a highly successful manner (Fig. 8). Jelliff, around the middle of the century, was producing comfortable upholstered furniture in the Gothic style (see Ill. 23). The chief furniture forms of the American Gothic revival were chairs, cabinet pieces, and beds.

The Elizabethan Revival Style. The style called Elizabethan in nineteenth century printed sources was popular at the same time as the Classical and Gothic styles—during the first half of the century. The chief characteristic of this furniture was a ball and spiral-twist turning that was actually borrowed not from the design vocabulary of the Elizabethan period but from the era of Charles I and Charles II. Writers during the nineteenth century often referred to any furniture produced before the middle of the eighteenth century as Elizabethan. The chief source of design inspiration for this style, however, was the Baroque period and the designs of the French designer Daniel Marot. Both Smith and Ackermann include designs for Elizabethan furniture in their books.

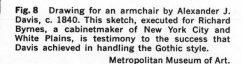

Downing shows such chairs in his *Architecture of Country Houses* (Fig. 9). Each of these examples is low to the floor with a high back resembling a *prie-Dieu*. In each the stiles are turned in the ball or spiral-twist manner. Such chairs often had elaborate needle-

Fig. 8 Drawing for an armchair by Alexander J. Davis, c. 1840. This sketch, executed for Richard Byrnes, a cabinetmaker of New York City and White Plains, is testimony to the success that Davis achieved in handling the Gothic style.
Metropolitan Museum of Art.

51

work upholstery·whose inspiration was from Baroque cushion
designs (see Ill. 21). While each of the Downing chairs has an
upholstered back and seat, it was often the practice to have an
elaborately carved and pierced openwork wooden back (see Ill.
24). The backs were carved with a great variety of intertwined
motifs also borrowed from Baroque sources.

The chief use of the Elizabethan style in the United States was
in a simple mass-produced type known as cottage furniture. In
such pieces the spiral twist was reduced to a simple ball- or spool-
turned straight member. This furniture was mass produced and
was highly advocated by Downing for country cottages because of
its practicality, attractiveness, and inexpensiveness. It was made
of a cheap softwood, painted and decorated in various colors, and
could be acquired with marble tops if desired. Many revival styles
were combined into a single set of cottage furniture; in one plate

Fig. 9 Three chairs in the Elizabethan revival style from Downing's *Country Houses.*
The chair to the right best demonstrates the·Baroque spiral-twist turning which is
most characteristic of this style, but the chair in the center shows the watering-down
of the turning into the more popular ball.

52

20 Side chair made of rosewood by Alexander J. Davis in New York, c. 1835. This masterwork by Davis is especially interesting because of the addition of the flattened cabriole leg and cloven foot to the Gothic back.

Museum of the City of New York.

21 Prie-Dieu made of rosewood, c. 1850. The Elizabethan form of turning as well as a modified type of Elizabethan needlework are to be seen in this chair; the Louis XV cartouche serves as an indicator of currents to follow.

William Hill.

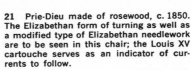

22 Bed of mahogany painted white, probably made in Philadelphia, c. 1833. This Gothic revival bed was given to Nicholas Biddle by Joseph Bonaparte and was used in a Gothic dependency at the former's house, "Andalusia."

Mr. & Mrs. James Biddle. Courtesy *Antiques*.

23 Side chair made of rosewood by John Jelliff of Newark, New Jersey, c. 1850. The open quatrefoil and well-carved crocket finial are important decorative Gothic details.

Newark Museum.

25 Chest of drawers made of painted pine and softwood, c. 1850. Applied split spindles of the Elizabethan revival style and painted decoration in the Rococo revival style are combined in this piece of cottage furniture.

Sleepy Hollow Restorations.

24 Slipper chair made of rosewood probably in New York, c. 1850. Baroque twist turning is demonstrated in the stiles and front legs of this piece; the interlaced splat is vaguely based on designs by Bérain.

Museum of the City of New York.

26 Side chair made of laminated rosewood by John H. Belter in New York City, c. 1850. The subdued scrolls and confined floral details indicate that this was one of Belter's early works.

Author's collection.

27 Slipper chair made of laminated rosewood by John H. Belter in New York City, c. 1855. The Rococo revival style is typified by the elaborate naturalistic carving of the back and the delicate scroll legs.

Author's collection.

from Downing's *Country Houses* a set is shown in which most of the pieces are Classical in shape, with the exception of a side chair and table which are Elizabethan, and all of the pieces are decorated in the Rococo taste (Fig. 10). Another Baroque decorative device, the application of split spindles to the front of a cabinet piece, was often used on cottage furniture (see Ill. 25). Occasionally the ball-turned pieces were made of a better wood and were more sophisticated in their conception. Among the most interesting pieces of American furniture of this type were nests of tables often made of mahogany or rosewood. With the exception of its use in cottage furniture, the Renaissance style, like the Gothic, never attained great popularity in the United States.

The Rococo Revival Style. Certainly the most popular of all revival styles in the middle of the nineteenth century was the Rococo. It probably had more intrinsic quality than any of the other styles, for while it was a new interpretation of eighteenth century Rococo of the court of Louis XV, the nineteenth century version still adhered to the earlier design vocabulary—the cabriole leg, curvilinear surfaces, S curves and scrolls, and shell carving. The Rococo style was referred to by contemporary writers as being in "the French taste" and "antique." This style is not truly a revival, however, because the cabriole leg had never completely disappeared from design sources of the late eighteenth and early nineteenth centuries in England, France, and the United States. In the 1840's design books began to appear in England which showed suites of this furniture and the fashionable Parisian cabinetmakers of that time had already revived the Louis XV chair.

The revival cabriole leg sometimes terminated in an S scroll toe and at other times in a straight cylindrical manner. The rear leg, instead of being cabriole in the Louis XV manner, was formed of a reverse curve chamfered at the termination to give a sense of

Fig. 10   A bedroom suite from Downing's *Country Houses*, of the painted cottage variety which was much advocated by this American tastemaker. He was impressed by its beauty, durability, and inexpensiveness.

solidity to the piece. The scrolls were interpreted in a heavier manner and the naturalistic carving of flowers, fruits, birds, etc., was given a lacy quality when it was incorporated into the overall design of the piece. Great improvements in mechanical techniques led to factory production of S and C scrolls and other carved ornament by the factory method. The Rococo revival style, more than any other popular at mid-century, is characterized by the mass production and dissemination of cheapened versions along with the production of superior examples by some of the most skilled craftsmen of the century.

Downing was a great enthusiast for the "Antique French" style and felt that it should be used chiefly in parlors and boudoirs because of its lightness of form. In a grouping of three side chairs in his *Country Houses,* Downing includes one with straight turned legs—a modification of the Louis XIV style (Fig. 11). This is a prelude to the short popularity of the style of the court of Louis XIV which will be discussed later in this section. Samuel Sloan included a very valuable section on furniture in his *Homestead Architecture* (Philadelphia, 1867). In this he honestly confessed to being confused by the design terminology of the suites of fur-

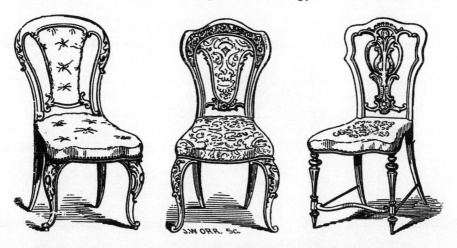

Fig. 11   Three side chairs from Downing's *Country Houses* in the Rococo revival style. The examples at left and center have the cabriole legs characteristic of this style, while the example to the right has front legs with Baroque turning.

57

Fig. 12 A suite from Sloan's *Homestead Architecture* is conceived in a more exacting interpretation of the Louis XV style.

niture which he illustrated. One suite, however, in which the seat furniture was upholstered in Gobelins tapestry, was certainly in the Rococo taste (Fig. 12). It contained a sofa, armchair and side chairs, center table, and elaborate *étagère*. He included another curious suite which was called "Antique Furniture" (Fig. 13); the five pieces shown are an unusual blending of the Classical and Rococo styles and the two chairs are described as "late importation from one of the best establishments of Paris."

Fig. 13 Sloan's *Homestead Architecture* considered this suite to be in the Louis XVI revival style, but it is obvious that other design idioms were also involved.

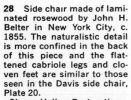

28 Side chair made of laminated rosewood by John H. Belter in New York City, c. 1855. The naturalistic detail is more confined in the back of this piece and the flattened cabriole legs and cloven feet are similar to those seen in the Davis side chair, Plate 20.

Sleepy Hollow Restorations.

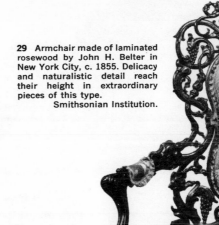

29 Armchair made of laminated rosewood by John H. Belter in New York City, c. 1855. Delicacy and naturalistic detail reach their height in extraordinary pieces of this type.

Smithsonian Institution.

30 Center table made of laminated rosewood by John H. Belter in New York City, c. 1860. The floral detail is closely confined so that the overall effect is of the Renaissance revival style.

Henry Ford Museum.

31 Bed made of laminated rosewood by John H. Belter in New York City, c. 1860. Beds were probably the most extraordinary creations of Belter's career. His last stylistic period—the Renaissance revival—is shown in this work.

The Brooklyn Museum.

32 Side chair made of mahogany, c. 1860. The balloon back was probably the most standard form of mid-19th century chairs.

Sleepy Hollow Restorations.

33 Dressing table of rosewood made by Prudent Mallard in New Orleans, c. 1860. This elaborately carved Rococo revival dressing table was made for "Lansdowne" at Natchez, Mississippi, where it is still in use.

Mr. & Mrs. George W. Marshall & Mrs. Singleton Gardner.

Probably the most famous name associated with American Rococo revival furniture is John Henry Belter (1804-1863). He received his training in Württenberg, Germany, migrated to New York and was first listed in the *Directory* of that city in 1844. He had numerous business addresses, the last on Third Avenue near 76th Street. Belter replaced Duncan Phyfe as New York's most fashionable cabinetmaker. Since some of his greatest contributions to furniture design were technical, Belter might well be discussed later in this chapter under the topic of progressive techniques. However, because of his effect on Rococo design, his technical innovations as well as his furniture will be discussed here.

The delicate, intricate, and lacy quality of carving in Belter's furniture could only have been done from a piece of laminated wood; an ordinary board would never stand such carving. Belter did not invent lamination; the Egyptians had been aware of it and constructed the tops of sarcophagi from panels of laminated wood. Belter's process consisted of gluing thin layers of wood (rosewood, oak, ebonized hardwood, about 1/16″ thick) together so that the grain of a given layer ran in an opposite direction from that on either side. The average number of layers was from six to eight although it sometimes varied from three to sixteen. The unusual part of Belter's process was that he steamed laminated panels in molds, or "cawls" as he called them; by this process he achieved great undulating curves. Another feature which distinguished Belter's work was the application of pieces of solid wood to the frame for extra ornament.

It might be said that the evolution of Belter's style went from a looseness of form in the late 1840's and early 1850's, with a strong statement of the Louis XV style, to a tightness and shapeliness from the mid 1850's until his death when the Louis XIV, Louis XVI, and Renaissance styles were dominant. Some of his earliest pieces had backs composed completely of entwined scrolls.

This was later modified; and although the scrolls were still highly important, there was some carved decoration (see Ill. 26). In the elaborate backs of his slipper or *prie-Dieu* chairs Belter approached the next period of his style; these were made up of elaborate entwined vine, floral, and fruit motifs which were enclosed in elaborate scrolls (see Ill. 27). Following this came pieces in which the scrolls had virtually disappeared and the naturalistic detail became dominant (see Ill. 29). With the beginnings of the Louis XVI style the design became completely balanced and the legs took on a straighter form (see Ill. 28). Belter applied for several patents for his laminating and steaming process. Few signed pieces of Belter's work survive, a notable exception being a rosewood center table with marble top which bears his label (see Ill. 30). A specific patent was taken out for a highly elaborate bed in the Renaissance taste, which is now in the Brooklyn Museum (see Ill. 31).

There were many imitators of Belter who were active in New York and other cities at the time. Charles A. Baudoine of New York was important among these. A manuscript notebook, apparently in the hand of a cabinetmaker named Ernest Hagen, which is now preserved in the Library of The Henry Francis du Pont Winterthur Museum, tells how Baudoine infringed on Belter's patents. Instead of forming the chair back from a single panel, as Belter did, Baudoine ran a seam down the center of the back.

Another cabinetmaker who worked in laminated furniture was George Henkels of Philadelphia. Some of the other important Rococo revival cabinetmakers were August Jansen, the Meeks Brothers, Alexander Roux, Leon Marcotte, and Gustave Herter in New York, Daniel Pabst and Gottlieb Volmer in Philadelphia, François Seignoret and Prudent Mallard of New Orleans, and S. S. Johns of Cincinnati (see Ill. 33).

Across the United States there were craftsmen producing fur-

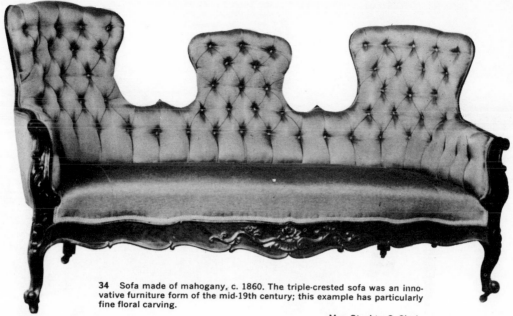

34 Sofa made of mahogany, c. 1860. The triple-crested sofa was an innovative furniture form of the mid-19th century; this example has particularly fine floral carving.

Mrs. Stephen C. Clark.

35 Sofa with an ebonized and gilt frame, probably made in New York City, c. 1860. Gilt rosettes and incised lined detail are characteristics of high style furniture of the Louis XVI revival.

Miss Caroline Rutter.

36 Side chair made of walnut, probably in New York, c. 1890. Sets of furniture in a more correct interpretation of the Louis XVI styles, were very popular near the end of the century.

Mr. & Mrs. John H. Kerr.

37 *Méridienne* made of mahogany, c. 1860. This furniture form is another innovation of the 19th century which is more commonly seen in the Classical rather than the Louis XV revival style.

Sleepy Hollow Restorations.

38 Armchair made of walnut with gilt decoration in New York City, c. 1860-1870. A mixture of Renaissance and Classical details makes this chair a curious eclectic example.

The Brooklyn Museum.

39 Side chair stamped "G. Hunzinger, N.Y., Patented 30 March 1869," and made of walnut. The principle of the folding chair is included in this stationary example, which is decorated with such typical Renaissance details as the acorn, incised floral motif, and ebonized bosses.

Author's collection.

niture in the Rococo revival style. Some of this was carefully created by hand while other pieces were machine-made and clumsy. Probably the most universal chair form was the side chair with "balloon back"; these were produced in enormous quantities in every part of the land (see Ill. 32). Another chair which became popular was a variant of the "balloon back" shape in which almost all of the back members were upholstered-over. This chair was sometimes expanded to create a triple-crested sofa with deep and undulating lines, a design originated in the nineteenth century (see Ill. 34). The sofa became a subject of increasing experiment around the middle of the century. Sometimes short versions of the *méridienne* type of the early century were made (see Ill. 37).

Another revival which paralleled the Rococo in development during the mid-century was the "Louis Quatorze" or "Modern French" style. This style was closely related to the neo-Baroque with its broken pediments, elaborate heroic figures, and geometric detail. The displays at the London Crystal Palace Exhibition of 1851 and New York Exposition of 1853 abounded with furniture of this type. Downing mentions that this style was in high esteem, and Sloan shows several illustrations of furniture suites in this taste in his *Homestead Architecture*. One of these (Fig. 14) shows the typical furniture form of the style—the sideboard with dripping garlands of fruit and flowers (and often carved game animals) crowned by an architectural pediment. The chairs and table included are in a simplified version of the style. Another plate (Fig. 15) shows a parlor suite in which the richly carved pediment reaches an extravagance of detail. The Baroque crests on the chair and sofa cresting rails, the broken arch pediment on the *étagère* and use of the decorative urn on the center table are all typical of the style. Because of the massive and rather clumsy proportions, very few examples of this furniture remain today because there is no space in the modern interior to accommodate it.

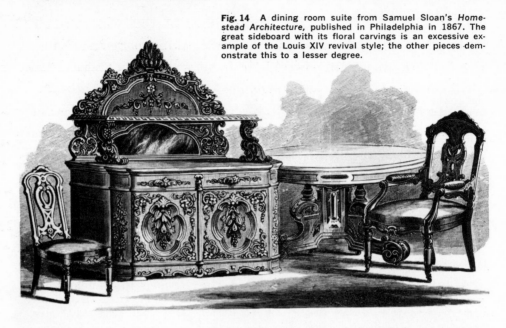

Fig. 14 A dining room suite from Samuel Sloan's *Homestead Architecture,* published in Philadelphia in 1867. The great sideboard with its floral carvings is an excessive example of the Louis XIV revival style; the other pieces demonstrate this to a lesser degree.

Historical Revivals, 1865-1900. The last thirty-five years of the century witnessed an increased widening of the scope of revivalism. By this time virtually every historic period was called upon for design inspiration and many different design sources would be incorporated into a single piece of furniture. Novelty was the keynote of the time, and designers vied with one another to produce more elaborate and showy pieces.

Fig. 15 This plate from Sloan's *Homestead Architecture* shows a curious late and misunderstood group of furniture intended to be in the Classical revival style.

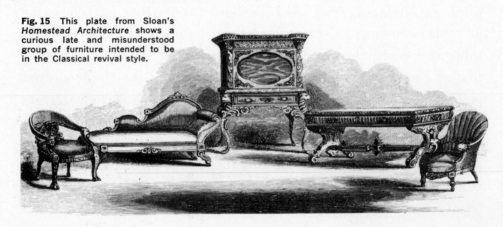

40 Cabinet made of rosewood and kingwood with tulip and ebony wood inlay by Léon Marcotte in New York City, c. 1875. The Renaissance architectural style with its contrasting dark and light surfaces and decorative detail is well incorporated in this piece.

Newark Museum.

41 Bedroom suite made of walnut veneer by Berkey & Gay Company of Grand Rapids, Michigan, c. 1876. The Renaissance style was popularly rendered at Grand Rapids in examples which were often ponderous and overworked in their detail.

Grand Rapids Public Museum.

One of the important revival styles of the time was the Louis XVI, which once again introduced straight lines and the straight turned leg into the design vocabulary. Its inception apparently dates from the 1850's when in France Empress Eugénie began to restore the private apartments of the palaces of the Tuileries and St. Cloud. She identified herself with the unfortunate Marie Antoinette, so it was only natural that these apartments should be furnished in Louis XVI revival furniture. She commissioned the German-born Parisian cabinetmaker George Grobé to execute a number of elaborate desks with inset painted porcelain plaques and extraordinary ormolu mounts. It was such pieces which inspired the vogue for Louis XVI revival furniture in London and New York, for they were imported by furniture houses in both cities.

American pieces are characterized by the use of oval backs and straight stiles, arm supports, and legs. Mahogany was the popular wood although it was often ebonized; decorations such as bow knots, Classical medallions, and delicate tracery were borrowed from the repertory of Louis XVI design. These motifs were inlaid with mother-of-pearl, ebony, and holly. Some of the most elaborate American pieces also had inset porcelain plaques while the typical variety, made along the Eastern seaboard, had an ebonized frame, with incised gilded decoration (see Ill. 35). In the 1860's cabinetmakers such as Jelliff of Newark and Henkels of Philadelphia turned their attention from Rococo revival furniture and began to produce Louis XVI pieces. New York was a center for their manufacture by such cabinetmakers as Léon Marcotte, Thomas Brooks, the Sypher firm, and Christian and Gustav Herter. Louis XVI revival furniture continued to be made into the 1880's and 1890's; these later examples were often more directly in imitation of French models (see Ill. 36).

The Renaissance revival style was another which was very

popular in the concluding years of the century. The Crystal Palace exhibitions in London (1851) and New York (1853) showed furniture in this style. Its exact source is uncertain but design books as early as the late 1830's included furniture in the "Cinque-Cento" or "French Renaissance" styles. Downing mentions it as being popular, along with the other revival styles, in 1850. Typical motifs of the style were the rounded or broken-arch pediment (often combined with a cartouche), the use of sculpturesque crests and busts, applied medallions, acorn trimmings, and the tapering baluster leg. Walnut and mahogany were the preferred woods and elaborate surfaces were produced on cabinet furniture through the use of burled panels.

Renaissance chairs could combine elements of the style in a heavy, massive manner (see Ill. 38) or they could be much lighter in their interpretation. G. Hunzinger, a New York cabinetmaker of German birth, produced some of the finest examples of this latter type (see Ill. 39). He had actually patented a folding chair in 1866 and when he also produced stationary pieces, they had much the same construction as the folding examples.

Often the greatest virtuosity of the cabinetmaker was to be observed in cabinet furniture. Certainly one of the greatest of these pieces was a large rosewood and mahogany cabinet produced by Léon Marcotte in New York about 1875 which incorporated virtually the entire Renaissance design vocabulary (see Ill. 40). The Renaissance style was popularized for the entire nation at Grand Rapids, Michigan. Here machine-made versions were turned out in enormous quantities; the elements of design became heavy and flattened and the product was often cheapened. An imposing bedroom suite of this type was made by Berkey & Gay Company of Grand Rapids for showing at the Centennial Exhibition in Philadelphia in 1876 (see Ill. 41).

During the 1870's antique collecting took on great momentum.

No longer exclusively the pursuit of the wealthy, the craze began to affect the middle class, who were now advised that the use of old Japanese screens and Spanish chairs could do much to improve interiors. However, even more important than this was the revival of interest in the furniture of the American colonial period. Certainly the Centennial Exhibition of 1876 did much to focus the eyes of the American public on the past. At the Exhibition there was a colonial kitchen and a set of furniture made from one of the oldest trees in Philadelphia. It had previously been thought that reproduction Queen Anne, Chippendale, and Classical furniture began to be made at this time and that it was shown at the Exhibition. Because of this, the name "Centennial" has long been associated with furniture of this type. In an exhaustive study of the Exhibition, Rodris Roth of the Smithsonian Institution has proved that no furniture of this type was shown in 1876 and that "reproductions" of such furniture were never produced in any great quantity until the very end of the century (unpublished speech). The importance of the Exhibition was in focusing attention on the past and it did eventually lead to the production of colonial revival furniture, more an Edwardian than a Victorian outgrowth.

One of the most curious revivals of the 1880's and 1890's was a renewed interest in Orientalism which took its inspiration from the Near East. It was a return to the same exoticism which had led John Nash to create the Royal Pavilion at Brighton for the Prince Regent during the first quarter of the century. The Moorish or Saracenic taste existed to some extent during the entire century. It was to be seen in both interior and exterior architecture, of which one of the most elaborate examples was P. T. Barnum's mansion "Iranistan," which was built in Bridgeport, Connecticut, in 1848.

Several tastemakers of the day advised that the Moorish style should be used only in smoking rooms. However, the "Turkish Corner" eventually was approved for any room of the house; it was composed of a Moorish divan set among Oriental rugs and cushions, the whole being contained under a tent-like cover. Such objects as brass trays on folding bases, Koran stands, wooden chests, and small screens were imported from the bazaars of the Near East for use in "Turkish Corners" (see Ill. 114). When seat or cabinet furniture was needed, standard revival forms were used but these were generally further decorated with Moorish ornament (see Ill. 44). Coil springs came into popular use at this time and comfort was of primary importance. The coil spring will be discussed as a progressive trend later in this chapter. The art of the upholsterer completely dominated furniture of this type and the efforts of the cabinetmaker were often obscured by the elaboration of the tufting, fringes, tassels, and embroideries. In a few instances complete rooms were fitted out by decorators in the Moorish style, the interior architecture, furniture, and decorative accessories all *en suite*.

Furniture shown at the Chicago Columbian Exhibition of 1892 revealed what had happened to furniture by the end of the century. All of the revival styles were represented from a totally debased version of the Classical revival of the beginning of the century to the Moorish of the end. In many instances these were so hopelessly mixed in a single piece of furniture that it was virtually impossible to distinguish the original source. Electicism and a definite decline of good design typify revival furniture at the end of the century.

Cabinetmaking Techniques. Since revival furniture was generally made of wood and produced in a cabinetmaker's shop, it would seem feasible to discuss the methods of construction here before

42 Cabinet of painted wood with inset paint-ed panels made by the Art Workers Guild of Providence, Rhode Island, c. 1894. The paint-ings were done by Charles W. Stetson and the carving probably was done by Sydney Bur-leigh, both of whom were members of the Guild.

Edgar Kaufmann, jr.

43 Armchair made of oak, by Henry H. Rich-ardson, Boston, c. 1878. This chair, designed for the Woburn (Mass.) Library, demonstrates Richardson's own interpretation of the Roman-esque style in furniture.

Museum of Fine Arts, Boston.

44 Armchair made of ebonized wood possibly in New York City, c. 1885. The Turkish style was used in a few complete rooms where all of the elements were designed *en suite*; this example, elaborately embroi-dered and fringed, was designed for the Rockefeller House at 4 West 54th Street, New York City.

The Brooklyn Museum.

going on to progressive furniture, which in many instances was made of materials other than wood. The most popular primary woods of the century were mahogany, rosewood, and walnut, with oak enjoying a brief vogue at the very end. Pines of various types and poplar were the most frequently used secondary woods.

The individual craftsman who conceived a piece of furniture and then executed it in the time-honored manner was still to be found. However, in great cabinetmaking shops, beginning with Phyfe in the 1820's, an assembly line method began to evolve. This distributed labor among the skilled and less skilled workmen; the skilled handled carving and the more complex construction procedures while the less experienced ran lathes and produced the simpler parts. Still another craftsman might combine the parts into a whole by actually constructing the piece of furniture. The shops of Meeks and Belter in New York carried on in the tradition of Phyfe. These, however, were certainly not factories with power-driven machinery in the modern sense. By 1861, Samuel Sloan mentions "steam factories" for making furniture in his *Designs for Rural Buildings*. This was the beginning of the power-machine era, which grew with increasing momentum during the remainder of the century. The great international exhibitions seemed to be dominated by halls of machinery and the machine greatly influenced the production and quality of inexpensive furniture. It might be well to remember that as early as 1840 John Hall was designing furniture primarily made of scrolls that could be cut on a bandsaw.

Indeed it was improvements in the saw more than any other tool which placed furniture under the domination of the machine. While the circular saw was known during the eighteenth century, it was not until the 1840's that it came into increased use. The advantage of this saw was that it could make very fine cuts; therefore thinner and larger sheets of veneer could be cut with it.

Thus it was possible to produce the enormous veneered surfaces which covered a soft secondary wood in large pieces of cabinet furniture. The development of the band saw was not so rapid and it was not until the 1850's that a satisfactory form of construction was discovered. Other power-driven improvements of the century were wood-carving machines, fret-cutting machines, and planing and mortising machines. Each of these was refined again and again before the end of the century and each was responsible in part for the production of quantities of inexpensive and ill-designed furniture during the second half of the century.

Design Reformers. The poor design, bad taste, and misuse of materials which were the result of the interaction of the machine age and historical revivalism began to be criticized by the mid-century. It was probably the exhibitions at the Crystal Palace Exhibition in 1851 which sparked this reaction. The decorative arts played an extremely important part in this exhibition and designers from many countries exhibited pieces in which the design motifs from numerous revival styles were mixed in a ponderous and inappropriate manner.

In England, Henry Cole (1808-1882), one of the organizers of the Crystal Palace Exhibition, spoke out strongly against the bad taste which was to be observed there. His *Journal of Design,* published from 1848 to 1852, was a prime force in early design reforms; he advocated the use of machinery in furniture making but urged restraint and good taste. A colleague of Cole's, Matthew Digby Wyatt (1820-1877) prepared a catalog called *The Industrial Arts of the Nineteenth Century: Illustrations of the Choicest Specimens of the Exhibition of 1851,* in which he compared the western products in confused revival styles to the simple and serene handcrafts of the Orient. Another reformer who shared these views was Owen Jones (1809-1874) who published *Grammar of Ornament* in 1856; many of the designs shown in this work were based on organic forms drawn from nature.

All of these early reformers were interested in the honest use of materials, controlling the overuse of ornament, and a return, in some measure, to handcraft methods in furniture making. The English art critic John Ruskin (1819-1900) won a wide audience, in both England and America, during the 1850's and 1860's. He was interested in the principles of form and organization in nature and the incidental effect which man's observation of nature could have on an artifact when he worked with it. Architecturally, Ruskin and his followers strongly favored the Venetian Gothic.

One of the strongest protests against the machine came from William Morris (1834-1896) and the group of painters with whom he was associated. Morris had been trained in architecture but he turned his attention to furniture design in 1861 when he founded a company to offer the public furniture of good taste. Morris and his associates turned to the English Gothic of the thirteenth century for inspiration, but instead of literally imitating the grammar of Gothic ornament they were more concerned with its basic structure, line, and proportions. The furniture produced by the Morris firm, which was constructed and decorated completely by hand, was too costly for popular consumption so the basic principle of improving popular taste was somewhat defeated. Painters of the pre-Raphaelite school such as Edward Burne-Jones, Dante Gabriel Rossetti, and Ford Madox Brown were involved in painting and decorating furniture for the Morris firm.

The style of William Morris was first publicized by Bruce James Talbert (1838-1881) in his book *Gothic Forms Applied to Furniture* (1867). Although Talbert also advocated "the principle of economy combined with strength," the illustrations in his book show that he allowed much more decoration and surface detail on his furniture forms than did Morris. This book was reprinted in the United States in 1873 and 1877, but its chief influence seems to have been on interior and exterior architecture.

Possibly the chief popular exponent of good taste in the Morris manner was Charles Locke Eastlake (1836-1906). His work *Hints On Household Taste* (1868) went through many editions in England; it was first published in the United States in 1872 and subsequently was reprinted here throughout the remainder of the century. Eastlake was decidedly opposed to the revival styles and advocated instead furniture that was simple, straightforward, and early English in its style inspiration. Most of the illustrations in his book show pieces which were a simplification of the Morris and Talbert types; they were made of oak, and had simple, incised decorations.

The Japanese taste began to evolve in the 1860's because of the Japanese prints and textiles that were shown at the London Exposition (1862) and the Paris Exposition (1867). In England the architect Edward W. Godwin (1833-1886) decorated his house in a Japanese manner as early as 1862. The furniture he designed had very thin horizontal and vertical members, and cabinet pieces contained complicated shelf arrangements. With his attempt to incorporate the asymetric and delicate linear effects of Japanese architecture into contemporary western furnishings, Godwin founded the Aesthetic Movement which was favored by Oscar Wilde and became the butt for cartoonists of the day. Christopher Dresser (1834-1904) was also a designer in the aesthetic taste. His furniture was severely plain, functionally conceived, and made up of geometric parts.

The Arts and Crafts Movement was an outgrowth of the philosophy of Ruskin and the practices of Morris; it flourished from 1882 until about 1910. Guilds for craftsmen were formed in England to encourage the creation and exhibition of objects that emphasized a proper use of materials and workmanship. Although medieval decorative devices were often used, they were reduced in importance and floral details were more naturalistic. Some important English leaders of the movement were Walter Crane (1845-1915), Arthur H. Mackmurdo (1851-1942) and C. F. A. Voysey (1857-1941). The Arts and Crafts Movement turned to humble, handmade things, and brought about a revival of cottage crafts. In the United States this movement was not as thoroughly organized as its English counterpart, but craftsmen did band together at various centers. One of the most famous of these was the Roycrofters group which Elbert G. Hubbard (1856-1915) founded at East Aurora, New York. Printing and bookbinding were the principal interest of this group, but they also fashioned simple pieces of furniture for the houses in their community.

Another, more obscure group, whose composition was more like that of Morris and his followers, was the Art Workers Guild of Providence, Rhode Island. Here designers, cabinetmakers, and painters all combined their talents in the production of furniture. While the group contained a number of members, the most important were Charles W. Stetson, painter, Sydney Burleigh, cabinetmaker and carver, and John G. Aldrich, architect. A cabinet which is said to have been made for Mrs. Burleigh was conceived in an overall Renaissance form with inset paintings by Stetson (see Ill. 42).

An American architect who designed furniture of unusual originality and vitality was Henry Hobson Richardson (1838-1886). His furniture, which was made of oak, was integrated in both scale and style with the architectural setting for which it was intended (see Ill. 43). It was handcrafted and can be considered as an Arts and Crafts manifestation. A very late nineteenth century American outgrowth of this movement was the Mission style; its effect lasted into the early twentieth century. Oak was the favored wood of this style and it was fashioned into furniture which was both massive and rectilinear with very little ornament.

Innovative Furniture. Intense experimentation with machinery during the nineteenth century caused some designers and craftsmen to produce furniture which was highly innovative and even revolutionary. In some instances this developed as a technical innovation in furniture construction while in other cases some mechanical contrivance was actually incorporated into the furniture form. The technical innovations will be discussed first and the mechanical devices will follow.

Lamination was one of the important innovative forms in furniture construction. The work of John Henry Belter, America's chief practitioner of lamination, has been discussed in the section on the Rococo revival style. Another designer whose work was closely related to Belter's was Michael Thonet (1796-1871). He began to experiment in Germany and Austria with lamination and shaping by steam between 1836 and 1840. By 1850 Thonet had perfected a method of bending pieces of birch wood of varying sizes into highly fanciful shapes. His furniture was known as bentwood and its sinuous curves were often reminiscent of the Rococo revival style. One of the important ingredients of the design of this furniture was that all of the component parts of a single piece could be shipped unassembled and later put together with screws. Much of the bentwood furniture was made in Austria, but it was imported into the United States in great quantities and imitative pieces of lesser quality and sophistication were made here.

The development of pressing and molding machines during the first half of the nineteenth century made possible the virtuoso use of a material that had been confined to smaller articles during the early part of the century—papier mâché. This was a durable substance produced by pressing together ground paper pulp or strips of paper with glue under great pressure. The molded form was treated with numerous coats of heavy lacquer (often black) and the piece was decorated with gilt color and nacre decoration. Technological advances made possible the production of large, intricate, and highly elaborate pieces of furniture, many of which were shown at the Crystal Palace Exhibition. The major producer of papier mâché furniture was England, where the most famous firm was Jennens and Bettridge. It was also made in France, but appears to have been made only in the most limited quantities and forms in the United States at Litchfield, Connecticut. However, papier mâché was very important in the nineteenth century American home and great quantities of it were imported into the country.

Iron was another innovative material in furniture design which became very important during the century. By the 1850's the iron industry had expanded greatly and quantities of objects were being mass produced from molds. Iron and steel had been used in a limited manner during the eighteenth century for furniture construction and bracing. However, it was not until the nineteenth century that the great popularity for metal furniture began to develop. As early as 1833 in his *Encyclopaedia,* Loudon showed two extremely curious chairs which were to be fashioned from metal and wood (Figs. 16 & 17). These chairs were designed by a 23-year-old protégé of Loudon, Robert Mallet. They were intended for inns and cottages; the backs and arms (in Fig. 16) were cast in a single piece and the legs and supports were made from hollow gas tubing. The seats were wooden and the whole was put together with screws.

Hollow tubular chairs were being produced in France during the 1840's; the tube was often reinforced with a core of glue or plaster to lend durability. One of the most popular of all tubular chairs was the elaborate rocker which was being made during

Fig. 16 This armchair from Loudon's *Encyclopaedia* is a curious early example of easily assembled furniture. The seat and back are wooden, while the legs, arms, and connecting members are of iron.

Fig. 17 A side chair from Loudon's *Encyclopaedia* is easily assembled and disassembled, as it is made of iron and wooden members.

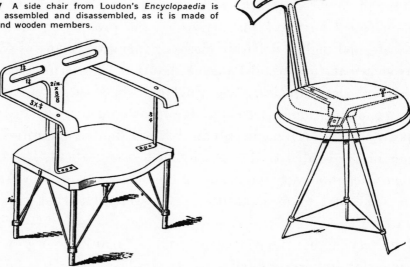

the late 1840's and 1850's; two bent pieces of metal tubing formed the entire substructure of the rocker. Another version of this chair had flattened metal members rather than tubes; an example of this type, thought to have been made by Peter Cooper, is preserved at the Cooper Union Museum in New York City.

The most popular metal furniture, however, was cast iron. It was made from an assemblage of parts cast in individual molds. This furniture was designed for both interior and exterior use and was often ornamental, with details drawn from one or more of the popular revival idioms. The form which has survived in greatest quantities today is the garden bench, which often combines a wood seat with an iron frame (Fig. 18). In many cases, a firm which produced iron furniture also made pieces from wire. Various new wiremaking machines made it possible to produce this highly adaptable material in much greater quantities and it could be twisted into highly elaborate and fanciful shapes (see Ill. 46). This furniture was generally intended for outdoor use.

45 Miniature armchair made of walnut, by G. N. Seidler and patented on February 20, 1877. This six-inch-high model incorporates all of the mechanism for adjustment and served as the patentee's application to the United States Patent Office.

William Hill.

46 Garden chair made of twisted wire, c. 1875. The Rococo revival style is applied here to what is essentially an innovative furniture form.

Henry Ford Museum.

47 Armchair with an iron frame marked "Sole M'frs./Marks A. F. Chair Co. Limited/930 B'way/Pat. Feb' 1st 1876." This chair can be adjusted from a stationary upright model to a completely flat bed.

Henry Ford Museum.

48 Side chair made of cast and wrought iron frame with japanned back, c. 1865. The give-and-take of the crown-shaped wrought iron base acts as a spring, so that this chair moves and reclines for the sitter.

Miss Elinor Merrell.

49 Armchair constructed with an iron rod support back with wire bundle springs, c. 1895. The upholsterer's art completely dominates in so-called "Turkish frame" furniture; the only wooden members are the legs and their connecting pieces.

Author's collection.

50 Armchair made from steer horns, c. 1885. This desk chair was presented to President Theodore Roosevelt by a Western admirer and well shows the inclusion of organic materials into a furniture form.

Sagamore Hill.

Fig. 18 Bench made of cast iron in the fern pattern, from the catalog of Hanson & Kirk, Philadelphia, 1874.

The other category of innovative furniture was that which incorporated some mechanical device in its makeup. Man had long been interested in movability and collapsibility in furniture; pieces from antiquity through the eighteenth century had in some instances incorporated devices for movability into their form. However, from the 1850's forward there was an increased interest in furniture which reclined, converted, and folded, and designers approached them with fresh enthusiasm. A reclining easy chair was shown in T. King's *The Modern Style of Cabinet Work* (London, 1832, [2nd Ed.]); the accompanying text stated "the back may be lowered by removing the stud (which goes through the brass plates projecting at the back), and placing it in a lower hole, thereby suiting the inclination of the back to the fancy" (Fig. 19). Hall's *The Cabinet Maker's Assistant* of 1840 showed a chair which could be converted to become a day bed. A type of folding chair

83

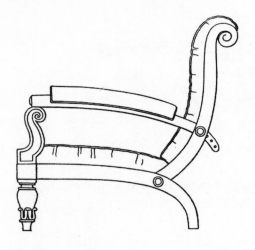

Fig. 19 A reclining easy chair, from *The Modern Style of Cabinet Work* published in London in 1832. The reclining back could be lowered by removal of the stud and thus be adjusted to the individual wish of the owner.

Fig. 20 A folding chair, from Gervase Wheeler's *Rural Homes*, published in New York in 1852, is the prototype of a chair that has become known as the director's chair in the 20th century. It is made of wood and canvas with metal fasteners.

was developed in the mid-century which has been popular since. It consisted of wood members supporting a canvas back and seat and an X-shaped wood base (Fig. 20). Today the term "director's chair" has been applied to this type. Hundreds of varieties of folding and convertible chairs were patented from the 1860's until the end of the century (see Ill. 47). Miniature models of furniture forms of this type were produced for the United States Patent Office before the patent was granted (see Ill. 45). Barber and dental chairs as well as beds and chairs on trains and steamships combined such contrivances into their makeup.

One of the greatest mechanical innovations in furniture design during the century was the widespread introduction of the metal coil spring. Sheraton had included a riding exercise horse in his *Cabinet-Maker and Upholsterer's Drawing-Book* (1793) which incorporated the use of coil springs upon which the rider was to bounce up and down. However, the coil spring was not introduced as a major innovation in creating comfort in furniture until the mid-nineteenth century. Because of the spring, the upholsterer's trade could triumph, for pieces were now designed in which the springs and their necessary upholstery were dominant.

The style for this comfortable furniture was set in France but it quickly migrated to England and the United States. Tufting, buttons, and fringes became its major symbols, and new forms such as the circular ottoman and easy chair began to develop. Loudon showed a circular ottoman in his *Encyclopaedia* (1833) but springs are not specified and it is doubtful that they were involved (Fig. 21). It is, however, the form which persisted until the end of the century. This incorporation of springs into furniture finally brought about a form in which the structure of the piece was invisible and only the upholstery could be seen. This was the Turkish frame type in which the entire form was made from wire bundles and then completely upholstered. A closely related type was called iron-back upholstering. Although the base of such a piece was composed of wire bundles, thicker iron rods formed the support for the frame above the seat level (see Ill. 49). (see also Ill. 122.)

A centripetal spring chair was shown in the United States section of the Crystal Palace Exhibition. It was patented by the American Chair Company of Troy, New York, a firm which was

Fig. 21 Circular ottoman, from Loudon's *Encyclopaedia*. This is an early statement of the art of the upholsterer which eventually found its fulfillment in furniture at the end of the century.

Fig. 22 This centripetal spring chair was patented by the American Chair Company of Troy, New York, in 1849. The engraving is taken from *The Illustrated Catalogue of the Great Exhibition* (1851).

well known for making reclining railroad car seats (Fig. 22). The catalog of the exhibition commented: "These chairs are constructed in a style peculiarly American. The arrangement of the springs beneath, and the almost universal movement of which they are capable, are new features in their manufacture." (See Ill. 48.) (See also Ill. 121.)

Furniture of Organic Materials. In contrast to the furniture produced under the influence of mechanization, the pieces produced from organic materials were principally made by hand. This furniture was generally intended for country retreats and outdoor use, where picturesque effects should be achieved.

Especially popular was furniture made from rustic wood; in such pieces tree branches and roots were combined to form a natural seat or table. Such furniture was made during the eighteenth century and an early nineteenth century source devoted to it was M. Taylor's *Ideas for Rustic Furniture Proper for Garden Seats, Summer Houses, Hermitages, Cottages, etc.* (London, 1838). In the United States, Downing, in his *Cottage Residences* (New York, 1844) illustrated a rustic garden bench and stated that "rustic seats, placed here and there in the most inviting spots, will heighten the charm, and enable us to enjoy at leisure the quiet beauty around." To create such a bench branches were carefully chosen so that they would naturally form the contours of

86

the piece. *The Horticulturist,* a periodical originally founded by Downing, carried two articles on rustic furniture in 1858 (Fig. 23). One of these stated: "An old apple or pear orchard furnishes capital materials; all that is required for their construction is a saw, an axe, a gauge, and a few nails. The requisite skill is possessed by every man of ordinary intelligence."

Fig. 23 *The Horticulturist,* a periodical originally founded by Downing, published two articles on rustic furniture in 1858. The magazine stated that it was a popular furniture form which could be made by anybody with a little imagination and a few tools.

Another organic substance extremely popular during the century was cane (wicker or rattan). The cane was the durable stem and tendril of a climbing palm which grew in the East Indies. The frames around which the steamed cane was woven were made from white oak or hickory. Cane was imported into New York in great quantities via Antwerp, Bremen, and Rotterdam. Accounts in Wheeler's *Rural Homes* (1852) prove that it was a going industry in New York. Three to four hundred boys at the House of Refuge as well as two thousand girls in the Bloomingdale section and in the suburbs were employed in cane manufactories. Wheeler illustrated a number of pieces among which the most interesting was a group of four (Fig. 24). About these he stated:

> The articles grouped together in our illustration exhibit a sofa, arm-chair, rocking-chair, and foot bench; the sofa, from the pointed termination of its curves approaching to the Gothic principle of construction; and the other pieces, from their symmetrical and rectilinear and spherical lines, adopted to an Italian or any other description of finish but the strictly Gothic.

Closely related to cane furniture was that made from bamboo. This was often in the Oriental manner, the frame made of bamboo

Fig. 24 A suite of cane furniture from Wheeler's *Rural Homes* demonstrates the inclusion of historical revival detail in an organic furniture form. The triple-crested sofa incorporates Gothic detail.

and the seat and back covered with woven cane. An elaborate reclining chair of this type was shown (Fig. 25) in Clarence Cook's *The House Beautiful* (New York, 1878).

Possibly the most exotic of all organic furniture was that made from natural animal horns. The vogue for antlers and other hunting trophies extends into antiquity, and furniture forms were being constructed of such material in the late eighteenth century. In the United States the western movement gave great impetus to an interest in steer and buffalo horns. A trade card which is preserved at the Smithsonian Institution states that William Thompson of 382 Washington Street, New York, was awarded "First Premium at the New Jersey State Agricultural Fair, at Waverly, Oct. 1867" and a "Diploma at the Morris Co. Fair, at Morristown, N. J., 1867" for his buffalo hat rack; this was described as "the lightest and handsomest hat rack ever made." Animal horn furniture was considered the proper souvenir for American presidents by Western admirers. Abraham Lincoln received an elk horn chair from a Western trapper and Theodore

Roosevelt's home "Sagamore Hill" at Oyster Bay, Long Island, still contains several horn chairs that were presented to him (see Ill. 50).

Collectors' Notes. The collector should be thoroughly familiar with the development during the nineteenth century of revival styles and furniture forms. This can be accomplished through a careful study of the good collections that exist at such institutions as The Brooklyn Museum, New York, Henry Ford Museum, Dearborn, Michigan, or "Fountain Elms," Utica, New York. In addition, the Bibliography at the end of this book will lead the collector

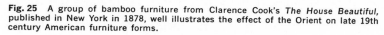

Fig. 25 A group of bamboo furniture from Clarence Cook's *The House Beautiful*, published in New York in 1878, well illustrates the effect of the Orient on late 19th century American furniture forms.

to sources that provide more information about specific aspects of each topic that might be of particular interest.

After one has acquired the ability to recognize the broad category into which a piece of furniture falls, one must then learn to examine the piece for its special features. Quality is chief among considerations. The piece of furniture must first of all be considered in terms of style. Is it a high-style piece which adheres to the general pattern books or sources of the nineteenth century, or is it the work of some individual who conceived it purely from his own point of view? Thus, one must distinguish high-style or urban-produced furniture from country-made pieces. Often the high-style piece is characterized by the use of a fine wood, the crispness and delicacy of carving, inlay, and other detail, masterful joinery, and overall good lines and proportions. The piece of country furniture is generally made from a native wood and often from a soft wood, carving and inlay are minimized or do not exist at all, the joinery methods are often conspicuous in the appearance of the piece, and the proportions are inspired by the individual whims of the craftsman.

Curiously enough, however, in the twentieth century, pieces of country make are often as desirable as those of the more sophisticated type. A cult of the primitive has arisen and simple country pieces are valued for the honesty and integrity of the craftsmen who produced them. In general, it is best for the collector to decide which area interests him, for the sophisticated and primitive do not often look well side by side. A thorough knowledge of style development is necessary for the collector of primitives, however, for only through this is it possible to determine the inspiration from which the design for an individual piece has sprung.

At the present time, probably the most desirable of all nineteenth century furniture is that which fits into the progressive or innovative category. Because this furniture is the direct ancestor

90

of many twentieth century furniture forms, it is sought by modern designers and collectors as well as antiquarians. In recent years the furniture in this category has skyrocketed in price while the more conventional revival pieces have gone up less drastically.

Size is another factor in determining desirability. Massive and ponderous cabinet pieces in the Empire or Rennaissance revival styles are of little value today because few people have enough room to use them. Today, it is the small and delicate pieces which are in greatest demand.

The condition of a piece is another consideration. Is the piece structurally sound? Does it have replaced parts? It is complete? What is the condition of the finish? These are all important factors. If the upholstery is original and is still in usable condition, this is yet another point of interest.

51 Coffee pot of porcelain made by the William Ellis Tucker factory in Philadelphia, Pennsylvania, c. 1825-38. The polychrome and gilt romantic scenic decoration is typical of the later products of the factory.

Henry Ford Museum.

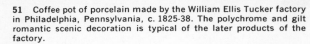

52 Pitcher of stoneware made by D. & J. Henderson of Jersey City, New Jersey, c. 1829-33. The raised hunt scene decoration was inspired by similar scenes found on many English pitchers of the time.

Henry Ford Museum.

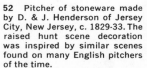

53 Pitcher of buff stoneware with a chocolate glaze, designed by Daniel Greatback and made by the American Pottery Company of Jersey City, New Jersey, c. 1838-45. The scene of the chase is typical of the period but the figure of the hound which forms the handle is particularly well molded.

Henry Ford Museum.

54 Pitcher of stoneware with a chocolate glaze, designed by Daniel Greatback and made by the American Pottery Company of Jersey City, New Jersey, c. 1838-45. English Gothic ornament of the apostles enclosed within Gothic niches is well applied to the body of this piece.

The Brooklyn Museum.

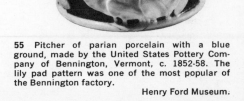

55 Pitcher of parian porcelain with a blue ground, made by the United States Pottery Company of Bennington, Vermont, c. 1852-58. The lily pad pattern was one of the most popular of the Bennington factory.

Henry Ford Museum.

Ceramics

Definitions. In any discussion of ceramics it is necessary to use a number of terms that are often confused. This chapter will therefore begin with a brief discussion of the most basic of these. There are essentially only three types of ceramics: pottery, semiporcelain, and porcelain. The often-used term "china" is synonymous with porcelain. The origins of this use arise from the fact that the first porcelain known to the western world came from the Orient and thus "china" became a common term for this ware.

Clay is the basic material for each type of ceramic, but pottery and semiporcelain are made from clay that contains impurities, while porcelain is made from clay that is refined and purified before firing. Porcelain is a finer ware and is usually white and translucent. Pottery is coarse; its body can be of many colors and is non-translucent. Semiporcelain is an in-between product that can take on characteristics of either pottery or porcelain.

The refined substance from which the body of a piece of porcelain is made is called paste. Hard paste is fine-grained, glossy in appearance, and is made from natural clay, while soft paste is porous and dull in appearance and is made from artificial clay. The glaze is the shiny material that covers the paste. The body can be thin and colorless (hard paste) or gummy and easily scratched (soft paste). Ceramics can be modeled by hand, they can be thrown on a wheel, or they can be made in molds. Sometimes a combination of these methods is used in producing a single piece. The glaze is applied at the time of firing at the kiln, and the body is often decorated before this process takes place so that the glaze will act to protect it. These are the basic factors and terms needed to understand ceramics; the vocabulary is endless, however, and other unfamiliar terms used in this chapter will be defined in the text or the glossary.

Early Porcelain. The story of the development of really fine American ceramics belongs almost exclusively to the nineteenth century. By 1800, the production of ceramics in the United States was virtually limited to pottery. If the manufacture of porcelain had been attempted before then, little is known about it today. During the eighteenth century, English ceramics were of great influence and American potters eagerly sought to imitate them. This continued to be the case during the early years of the nineteenth century, but French porcelains also became an important influence. They were imported in considerable quantities into this country and were eventually imitated quite successfully.

It was probably Dr. Henry Mead of New York who made the first actual American porcelain on an experimental basis in 1816. However, very little is known about this venture, for today only a single documented example of his work survives—a white soft paste vase in the Empire style with an urn-shaped body and caryatid handles. Many other attempts to produce porcelain quickly followed, especially in Philadelphia and in New Jersey, where the Jersey City Porcelain and Earthenware Company first produced examples in 1826.

It was in Philadelphia that American porcelain was first successfully produced in quantity; the name of William Ellis Tucker is the most famous in connection with this development. Tucker began to make his wares about 1825 and by 1827 his factory was in

56 Pitcher of porcelain made by Fenton's Works at Bennington, Vermont, c. 1845-47. Historical revivalism is to be observed in the Rococo naturalism of the raised ornament of this piece.

Henry Ford Museum.

57 Pitcher of earthenware with a light blue glaze, made by E. & W. Bennett of Baltimore, Maryland, c. 1849-56. This famous fish pitcher, with a sea monster forming the handle, is amusing but ill-conceived as a ceramic form.

Henry Ford Museum.

58 Classical male figure of buff earthenware with a white slip and brown painted decoration, made by Solomon Bell, Strasburg, Virginia, in 1862. While figures are common in English pottery, they are rarely seen in American ware.

Henry Ford Museum.

60 Vase of porcelain made by the Union Porcelain Works at Greenpoint (Brooklyn), New York, c. 1876-77. Organic naturalism is the chief characteristic of this charming small vase which is handsomely conceived.

Henry Ford Museum.

59 The Centennial Vase of porcelain which was designed by Karl Müller and made by the Union Porcelain Works at Greenpoint (Brooklyn), New York, in 1876. This vase was made for the Philadelphia Centennial and was to embody the spirit of American history, industry and art.

The Brooklyn Museum.

full production. The porcelain was of a high quality and carefully followed European models—French Empire examples being the most popular. The earliest pieces were undecorated, then gilt and sepia decorations were included, and finally elaborate floral decorations, figures, and scenes were painted in polychrome enamels (see Ill. 51). Some of the most interesting of the scenes show views of Philadelphia and its environs. The firm, which was in existence until 1838, went through a number of changes; after bearing W. E. Tucker's name alone it was Tucker and Hulm, Tucker and Hemphill, Joseph Hemphill, and Thomas Tucker. While not all of the pieces were marked, some bore the incised initials of W. E. Tucker, and still rarer are the painted inscriptions "William Ellis Tucker," "Tucker & Hulm," and "Joseph Hemphill." Today these are the only marks on Tucker's wares which have come to light.

Molded Pottery and Porcelain. About 1825 molded pottery began to become very popular. This was due to both improvements in machine technology and a change in public taste; pieces of this type were produced in large commercial potteries. Most examples were made from earthenware with a variety of glazes.

In 1828 David Henderson took over the Jersey City Porcelain and Earthenware Company which, as previously mentioned, made some porcelain about 1826. Henderson renamed it the American Pottery Manufacturing Company. The emphasis of the factory was on the imitation of English wares, and pottery of the Rockingham type was the most extensively produced. This had a heavy body with all-over bold raised design and generally a dark brown glaze. The firm also made stoneware, yellow ware, and creamware that was decorated by the transfer-printing method which had been perfected in England at the Staffordshire potteries. While tea sets were produced in creamware, the greatest output of the factory in other forms was pitchers. Some of these are as fine in design and execution as their English prototypes. The popular hunt pitcher was produced there in quantity in stoneware with clear and colored glazes (see Ill. 52). A variant of the hunt pitcher with a hound handle enjoyed great popularity at the factory.

One of the most important designers for the American Pottery Manufacturing Company was Daniel Greatback. He designed a hound-handled pitcher of great beauty as well as more original examples which borrowed heavily from English Gothic ornament (see Ills. 53 & 54). Marks on such pieces are generally impressed and they vary from "Henderson's Flint Stoneware/Manufactory, Jersey City" to "American/Pottery Co./Jersey City, N. J." This factory was active until the middle of the century.

Bennington, Vermont, became another important center for the manufacture of quality pottery and porcelain. Christopher Weber Fenton established Lyman, Fenton and Company at Bennington in the mid 1840's. By 1850 this firm had grown into the United States Pottery Company, which became nationally known for its mass-produced wares, consisting of a large number of utilitarian pieces of earthenware with various glazes. However, for more decorative objects, soft-paste porcelain and parian were used. (Parian is a pottery or porcelain left unglazed.) Parian pieces were often partially colored blue with a contrasting area left white, reminiscent of the famous blue and white vases of the Wedgwood Company (see Ill. 55).

Some of the mass-produced Bennington pottery was simple and unsophisticated, while other examples were highly imaginative and utilized all of the possibilities in molding techniques. Elaborate designs were modeled in the body of the piece as well as applied in fanciful decorative details (see Color Plate C). Designs utilized in the more decorative wares ran the historical revival gamut from Rococo pieces with highly involved naturalistic details to sym-

97

metrical pieces of Classic and Gothic inspiration (see Ill. 56). Wide recognition and praise were given to the products of this company, some of which were exhibited at the New York Crystal Palace exhibition of 1853. The United States Pottery Company was in operation until 1858; pieces can be identified by incised and stamped marks, the latter being more common. Early pieces (1845-50) are identified by "Fenton's/Works/Bennington/Vermont" while later examples (1850-58) are identified by a ribbon mark bearing the initials "U.S.P."

By the middle of the century there were also several famous potteries in the South. C. and W. Bennett of Baltimore, Maryland, established a firm in the late 1840's which continued in operation until 1856. This firm produced decorative earthenware pieces, often of an extremely naturalistic and clumsy design. To the eyes of the twentieth century the famous fish pitcher designed and produced by this firm appears highly amusing (see Ill. 57). The fish pitcher is made of majolica, a crude earthenware which is lead-glazed in many colors. These pieces are generally marked "E & W Bennett/Canton Avenue/Baltimore, Md." Majolica became a favorite material at this time and the Wedgwood cauliflower ware, whose richness of detail lent itself to this medium, was copied in this country by Carr and Morrison. Griffen, Smith, and Hill of Phoenixville, Pennsylvania, produced quantities of this majolica during the 1880's in such popular patterns as the maple leaf, shell and seaweed, and cauliflower.

A famous family of potters named Bell established themselves in Strasburg, Virginia, about the middle of the century. This prolific family produced a great variety of forms in earthenware that was less sophisticated than that produced by the northern factories. Among the rarities of this factory are the statues of humans which somewhat resemble the figures that were mass produced at the Staffordshire potteries (see Ill. 58). Members of the family continued to produce pottery into the third quarter of the century; pieces are often marked with "Bell" plus the first name of the potter and "Strasburg" with the date.

Porcelain, 1850-1900. One of several important centers for the manufacture of porcelain was at Greenpoint in Brooklyn, New York. A factory for the manufacture of soft-paste porcelain was opened there in 1847 by Charles Cartlidge, who had been trained in Staffordshire. This factory made decorative tableware as well as buttons and door hardware. Probably its most famous product was a pitcher whose body was composed of oak leaves and acorns with the raised design picked out in gold. This pitcher was designed by Josiah Jones, the most important modeler for the firm. A rare survival from this factory is a small paperweight with a reclining dog on a pillow which Cartlidge presented to Washington Irving for his house, "Sunnyside." Many of these pieces are unmarked, although "Greenpoint" sometimes occurs.

The Cartlidge factory closed in 1856, and then was operated briefly between 1857 and 1861 by William Bock and Brothers, who continued to produce the same general line. In the latter year the firm was taken over by Thomas C. Smith, who changed the name to Union Porcelain Works. The factory continued to make soft-paste porcelain until 1864, when hard-paste objects also began to be produced. At this time the real designer of decorative wares was the moldmaker, for the ideal of individual craftsmanship had almost completely disappeared. Form and decoration paid little attention to the properties of ceramics but rather followed the popular ideal of the day and often combined several elements in an outlandish way. Applied decoration had no relationship to the overall shape of the piece.

Sometime during the 1870's, Karl Müller, a sculptor, joined the Union Porcelain Company. It was he who was responsible for designing some of the most famous pieces of American porcelain. He was influenced strongly by the eclecticism of the day and his pieces have a sculpturesque quality which generally indicates little knowledge of the basic qualities of ceramics. One of Müller's famous early productions (about 1875) was a tea set in which the finials at the tops of the teapot and sugar bowl were modeled as the heads of a Chinese and a Negro. Rabbits and goats provided supports and handle terminations and the body of all pieces was decorated in a pseudo-Chinese manner with flowers, birds, and butterflies.

The most famous piece designed by Müller is "The Century Vase," which was made for the Philadelphia Centennial of 1876. In this vase Müller demonstrated his interest in minutiae and careful avoidance of a concept of the whole, for the piece is covered with painted and parian relief scenes that portray various aspects of American history and technological development. A medallion of George Washington, crowned by an American Eagle with thunderbolts, is the dominant decoration of the face of the piece; two bison heads provide handles on either side (see Ill. 59).

However, it is in some of the less pretentious pieces that the real genius of the Union Porcelain Company is to be seen. A surviving group of small vases have flaring organic tops and are supported by small animals or reptiles at the base. Not only are these pieces whimsical, but their design and execution are of the highest quality (see Ill. 60). Even utilitarian pieces produced during the 1880's were often of the finest quality and decoration. A water cooler, made in 1888, is perfect evidence of this, for the design conforms to the shape of the piece and does not attempt to obscure its practical nature. The Union Porcelain Company continued to produce until the turn of the twentieth century, giving it a very long life compared to other nineteenth century potteries. Pieces were often marked "Union/Porcelain/Works/Greenpoint

100

62 Dish in the shape of a swan, made by the Ceramic Art Company of Trenton, New Jersey, c. 1889-96. This was one of the famous products of the company, which eventually became Lenox, Inc., the most famous name in American porcelain.

The Brooklyn Museum.

61 Vase of Belleek porcelain made by Ott & Brewer Company of Trenton, New Jersey, c. 1883-92. Orientalism is the dominant theme in the raised polychrome decoration of this vase.

The Brooklyn Museum.

63 Clock case of Belleek porcelain made by the Willets Manufactory Company of Trenton, New Jersey, c. 1890. Porcelain clock cases were in vogue during the last quarter of the century and this example has especially fine and restrained decoration.

Henry Ford Museum.

64 Covered vase of Lotus ware (highly translucent and brittle porcelain) made by Knowles, Taylor and Knowles Company in Liverpool, Ohio, in 1897. Each of these pieces was the individual creation of a designer and decorator, and this ware ranks among the best porcelain made in America.

Henry Ford Museum.

65 Vase of glazed earthenware made by the Rookwood Pottery Company of Cincinnati, Ohio, c. 1900. The decoration of this piece is well suited to the shape and demonstrates the mastery of Rookwood designs.

The Brooklyn Museum.

/N. Y." with the date included; another familiar mark was "U.P.W." over an eagle's head whose beak grasped the initial "S."

Another important center for the manufacture of porcelain during the second half of the century was Trenton, New Jersey. One of its most important factories was Ott and Brewer Company, founded in 1863. A new body used in the early 1880's was Belleek, a very thin and translucent porcelain that was first developed in Ireland. Because of its high translucence, it lent itself to the production of vases and small dishes of a decorative nature. Ott and Brewer excelled in the production of Belleek and the decoration was frequently of great sophistication, often having an Oriental flavor (see Ill. 61). Typical marks are "Manufactured by/Ott & Brewer/Trenton, N. J., U. S. A.," and a crown pierced by a sword with "Belleek" above and "O & B" below.

The Ceramic Art Company was another famous Trenton firm; it was founded in 1889 by Walter Scott Lenox. This factory excelled in the production of Belleek and the swan dish of about 1890 was one of its most famous creations (see Ill. 62). The firm was renamed Lenox, Inc., in 1906 and is now renowned the world over. Typical marks are "The/Ceramic Art Co./Trenton, N. J." enclosed within a wreath, and a highly stylized "C A C" enclosed within an oval with a painter's palette and brushes to the left. Still another Trenton pottery which produced Belleek was the Willetts Manufactory Company. The most important pieces made at this factory during the late 1880's and 1890's are notable for the delicacy and restraint of their decoration (see Ill. 63). The typical mark was a snake coiled to form a "W" with "Belleek" above and "Willetts" below.

In 1872 a pottery was established in East Liverpool, Ohio. Its porcelain was destined to rank in importance with that of the factories at Greenpoint and Trenton. This was Knowles, Taylor and Knowles Company and their first product at that time was ironstone china or an earthenware with a granite glaze. However, in the 1880's they developed a porcelain as thin and translucent as Belleek which was called Lotus ware. Each of the pieces of this type was individually designed, executed, and decorated, a notable exception to the standard practices of the day. Oriental shapes were often quite evident in these pieces, although the decoration was generally the standard Rococo revivalism of the day (see Ill. 64). The usual mark was "Knowles, Taylor and Knowles" within a circle surrounding a crescent and star and "Lotus Ware" beneath the circle. The porcelain produced by this firm was among the best produced anywhere in the world at the time.

Art Pottery, 1870-1900. By the mid 1870's, the effects of William Morris's Arts and Crafts Movement were being felt in the United States. The ideals of handcraft which were inherent to the movement had a strong effect on ceramics, and potters now wished to create entirely new forms and to decorate them in an original manner. These artist-potters often taught the craft in the new schools that were springing up in the East and Midwest to train artisans.

One of the most important manifestations of this ideal was developed in Cincinnati, Ohio, in the formation of what was eventually to be called the Rookwood Pottery. In that city in 1874, Benn Pitman originated a class for teaching china painting to a group of prominent women. The class prepared a group of wares that were shown at the Philadelphia Centennial of 1876 and immediately brought forth high praise from the press and art critics. M. Louise McLaughlin continued to work with the group and eventually developed her famous "Losanti ware," a hard-paste porcelain fired at a low temperature and glazed with feldspar. Because of their highly vitreous quality, some of her pieces actually resemble glass. Losanti ware was exhibited at the Paris Exhibition of 1878, and the following year Miss McLaughlin founded the Pottery Club of Cincinnati.

A member of the club, Mrs. Marion Longworth Storer, founded her own pottery in 1880 which she called Rookwood after the Longworth estate. Mrs. Storer was a famous Cincinnati socialite and wife of the diplomat Bellamy Storer. By 1890, when Mrs. Storer retired, the factory was a successful business. In 1892 the factory was moved to a group of buildings high on a hill near the Cincinnati Art Museum, where it is still in limited operation.

Rookwood Pottery was strongly influenced by Orientalism, and its shape, decoration, and glaze were often testimonies to this fact. There was also the strong influence of naturalism, and the beginnings of *Art Nouveau* are to be observed in many of the pieces. Vases were the chief product of the factory; all pieces were unique and differences were even to be observed in pairs. Some of the most important decorators for Rookwood Pottery before 1900 were Albert R. Valentien, Matthew A. Daly, A. Van Briggle, E. P. Cranch, and a Japanese, Kataro Shirayamadani. Each piece was marked—from 1880 until 1882 the mark was an overglaze painted "Rookwood Pottery, Ohio," from 1882 to 1886 the impressed mark was "Rookwood" and the year, and finally in 1886 it became an impressed monogram "R P" and a sunburst with one additional ray being added for each year. The latter mark is still in use today.

Two other art potteries which developed during the last quarter of the century were the Weller Pottery at Zanesville, Ohio, and Hampshire Pottery which was established at Keene, New Hampshire, by J. S. Taft. Each of these produced wares which were similar to those made at the Rookwood Pottery. Individuality was stressed, but pieces sometimes lacked the subtlety of decoration and richness of color which was to be found in the work of their famous competitor.

A Armchair attributed to Maximilian Godefroy (fl. 1806-1824), made for the First Unitarian Church, Baltimore.

First Unitarian Church, Baltimore.

B Cast iron dressing glass in Rococo revival style with painted decoration, c. 1850.

Sleepy Hollow Restorations.

C Parian porcelain vase, possibly made in Bennington, Vermont, c. 1855.

Sleepy Hollow Restorations.

D Glass goblet, possibly made by Bakewell & Co. of Pittsburgh for President Monroe, c. 1817.

Henry F. du Pont Winterthur Museum.

E   Wicker Room at "Octagon House," Irvington-on-Hudson, New York, c. 1870.

Mr. and Mrs. Carl Carmer.

F   Parlor at "Irving Cliff," Irvington-on-Hudson, New York, c. 1867.

Miss Caroline Rutter.

G Drawing room of Princess Artchil Gourielli's apartment, New York City.

Princess Artchil Gourielli.

H Dining room at Washington Irving's "Sunnyside" at Tarrytown, New York, 1837-1859.

Sleepy Hollow Restorations.

Still another important development in pottery toward the end of the century was an increased interest in the design and decoration of tiles. About 1880 Chelsea, Massachusetts, became a center for tile manufacture. Hugh Robertson was among the earliest in the field, but the most famous tiles were created by John G. Low. He employed Arthur Osborne whose superior paintings in relief were instrumental in establishing Low's reputation. Tile painting became so popular that a group of leading artists banded together to form the Tile Club in New York.

Closely allied with the tile craze was the increased use of terra cotta tiles in architecture. Inspired by the search for a fireproof building material, such famous architects as Louis Sullivan, James Renwick, and Thomas Hastings designed ornaments to be incorporated into buildings. The more decorative tiles were used around doorways and windows while simpler examples were used in concealed structural areas. Some of the tiles designed by Sullivan came close in concept to the organic naturalism of *Art Nouveau*. These tiles were made at a great number of factories across the nation and molds and patterns were supplied to builders everywhere.

By the end of the century, mat pottery glazes were the rage. This glaze was generally a dull green color and the pottery was of a type which epitomizes in many minds today the bad taste of the nineteenth century. However uninspired the glaze might be, the forms to which it was applied were often of great interest, sometimes of great beauty.

William H. Grueby, who had been at the Boston Terra Cotta Company, introduced this glaze in 1894 and shortly afterward an identical glaze began to appear in other leading potteries. By 1900 the organic naturalism of *Art Nouveau* was beginning to achieve full expression in pottery and continued to be in vogue until about 1920. Pottery was one of the favorite mediums through which

American craftsmen expressed themselves in the *Art Nouveau* style.

The attempt in this account has been briefly to trace the development of high style American ceramics during the nineteenth century. It is to be remembered that throughout the period country potters continued to produce forms which are more easily identifiable with the eighteenth century. Thus, slip-decorated pottery continued to be produced well into the century as was red ware, yellow ware, and stoneware. Since these do not represent an original contribution to the century, but are rather a contribution of age-old trends, a discussion of these forms has been omitted.

Nineteenth Century Ceramics in the Twentieth Century. Since the ceramics of the nineteenth century have for so long been derided and lampooned by twentieth century critics, they offer a vast field as collectibles today. The fact that many ceramics are marked is a tangible aid to the beginning collector. Familiarity with any of the standard references on marks which are noted in the bibliography is essential to intelligent collection of American ceramics. For many years there has been a taste for Tucker porcelain and for the molded potteries of the first half of the century. However, the porcelains and especially the pottery of the second half of the century have been greatly neglected.

It is still possible to find excellent examples by most of the important porcelain factories. A small collection showing the evolution of style in porcelain would be of great interest. Much still needs to be known about the decorators of American porcelain and here, too, a modest collection, combined with curiosity and a bent for research, could produce some interesting results.

Because of a revival of interest in *Art Nouveau* about 1950, good examples of Rookwood have recently become more difficult to find. However, there is still enough available for the formation of a good collection. The important thing to remember in ceramics collecting is the conformity of the shape of the piece to the essential characteristics of the clay. If the designer of the vessel has had this in mind, the piece will be satisfying. While some pieces that violate this principle are at first highly amusing, they do not wear well.

66 a) Decanter and stopper, clear blown three-mold glass, c. 1825, Boston and Sandwich Glass Company. The pattern represented here is one of the Baroque group, of which a great number were produced at Sandwich.
b) Vase, opalescent blown glass, c. 1840, Boston and Sandwich Glass Co. This rare form has a fiery opalescence which is unusual in a piece of this date.

Sleepy Hollow Restorations.

67 Tumbler, clear blown molded glass, c. 1825, attributed to Bakewell & Page of Pittsburgh. The diamond and fan cutting was one of the earliest decorative devices found in Pittsburgh glass.

The Brooklyn Museum.

68 Salt, clear blown molded glass, c. 1825, New England Glass Company (Cambridge, Massachusetts). Salts of this type were among the first objects which were blown molded in a single mold.

The Brooklyn Museum.

69 Decanter, olive-green blown three-mold glass, c. 1830. Keene Glass Works (New Hampshire). The waffle and sunburst was one of the most familiar patterns of blown three-mold glass. One of the ridges created by the three-part mold may be seen to the right of the sunburst.

The Brooklyn Museum.

70 Sugar bowl with cover, amethyst blown glass, Ohio, c. 1820, following a form common to 18th century Pennsylvania glass. This is an example of the lag in style in glass forms made away from urban centers; the clown's hat cover is typical of mid-18th century forms.

The Brooklyn Museum.

Glass

Techniques and Definitions. Since early in recorded history, glass has been one of man's great miracles and most sought-after collectibles. Its skillful production requires the combination of the artistic abilities of the glassblower and the scientific skills of a number of workers in the glasshouse.

Silica, in the form of sand, forms the base for glass, together with certain proportions of potash, lead, and carbonate of soda, and small amounts of manganese and arsenic. When all of these ingredients are present and combined in the correct proportion, the product is called "flint glass" or "lead glass." When a piece of flint glass is struck, it responds with a bell-like ring. When lead is omitted from the basic ingredients, the product is called "soda-lime glass"; this responds with a dull sound when it is struck.

The desired mixture is prepared from bins of ingredients stored in the glasshouse. It is then placed in large clay pots and brought to white heat over a raging fire. At first wood was the only fuel available, but about the middle of the nineteenth century coal began to be used and, later in the century, natural gas. When the mixture reaches a completely fluid state, it is impossible to work, so it is allowed to cool to the temperature at which it can be blown or pressed.

Blowing glass is an art which requires great skill as well as the participation of several workmen. The master blower is known

109

as a "gaffer," and much of the work is done by him. An assistant first takes up the needed amount of molten glass, or "gather," on the end of an iron blowpipe. He forms the gather into the desired shape by rolling it on an iron table and then gives it to the gaffer, who inflates it and creates the form. Another assistant now brings a small glob of molten glass on the end of a "pontil" rod. This is applied to the swell of glass opposite the blowpipe and the gaffer breaks the entire shape away with a sharp tap. The gaffer works with the glass now attached to the end of the pontil rod and fashions it with simple wooden and metal tools. If the piece is complicated, it must be reheated again and again in the "glory hole," a special furnace for this purpose, or the glass quickly cools and becomes unmanageable. When the piece achieves its final form it is placed in an annealing oven for a day or so where the temperature is gradually decreased until the piece can withstand room temperature.

A refinement on free blowing is achieved by blowing into a mold. The mold may be of one or several parts and often has a pattern on the interior. The gather is lowered into the mold and then inflated, thus imprinting the pattern on the surface of the glass.

Certainly the great bulk of glass produced in the nineteenth century and, indeed, in the twentieth, has not been hand manipulated but has, rather, been made by machine. This is called "pressed" glass, and a greater degree of uniformity and standardization can be achieved through this process. Pressed glass is essentially an American innovation of the 1820's (its exact origins will be discussed later in this chapter). The process is essentially one of squeezing glass into shape under pressure. The interior of the mold is shaped to correspond to the desired exterior of the glass vessel. A glob of molten glass is placed into the mold, and a plunger squeezes the glass into place and provides a smooth surface for the interior of the piece. At first, glass-pressing machines were

71 Salt, opaque pressed glass, c. 1820; marked "New England Glass Company, Boston." Knobs and salts were among the first objects to be pressed and this single rectangular form, with its baskets of flowers, was one of the most successful of the early group.

The Brooklyn Museum.

72 Goblet, clear pressed glass, c. 1869, New England Glass Company. This goblet is from a pattern known as "Washington"; numerous table services were produced in this fine flint glass.

The Brooklyn Museum.

73 Goblet, clear pressed glass, c. 1875, Midwestern. This pattern, known as "Odd Fellow," was one of the intricate designs contrived to obscure the imperfections of soda-lime glass.

Henry Ford Museum.

74 Covered compote, clear and frosted pressed glass, c. 1880, Gillinders Company, Philadelphia. The frosting on the lion compote was produced by an acid; the frosted and clear patterns were among the most successful pressed glass.

Henry Ford Museum.

75 Wine glass, blown ruby overlay glass, c. 1855. Engraved by Louis Vaupel at the New England Glass Company; marked on base "LT–CH Pattern, No. 43, Vaupel, 239." The vintage pattern was borrowed from Bohemian glass and became the most popular of all overlay patterns.

The Brooklyn Museum.

turned by hand; this has been so completely revolutionized that today assembly line techniques turn out thousands of pieces a day.

It has generally been agreed that the best decoration a piece of glass can have is something intrinsic to the material itself. Thus glass applied to a glass body as decoration gives the same fluid quality as the basic material. However, there have always been consumers who wish more elaborate decoration; thus cutting, engraving, etching, and enameling have long been popular methods although they have nothing to do with the art of glassmaking.

Cutting is accomplished by holding the glass against a copper wheel over which a mixture of sand and water is running. This is followed by polishing on wheels of sandstone and wood. Engraving is a similar process, but the wheel is smaller and the solution is of oil and emery powder. Etching is a process that often imitates cutting; the background of the piece is covered with wax and the free area or design is coated with a solution of hydrofluoric acid which eats away the desired pattern. Enameling is painting on glass with colors that are themselves semi-vitreous; the whole piece is then fired.

Blown and Blown Molded Flint Glass. By 1800 there were not only glasshouses all along the eastern seaboard, but they had begun to spring up in the Midwest. In these midwestern factories, styles often lagged behind those of the East so that forms which are more identifiable with the eighteenth century were in standard production during the first quarter of the nineteenth. Ohio was a chief center of the midwestern glass industry; objects were produced there by the blown and blown molded methods (see Ill. 70). This glass was never made in great quantities, for it could not compete with the fine glass being imported from England and Ireland.

Because of this, the production of flint glass was at a virtual standstill at the turn of the century.

It was in Pittsburgh, in 1807, that the flint glass industry was reestablished, when two Englishmen began to construct a glasshouse. The initial attempt was not successful, but in 1808 the project was brought to completion by Benjamin Bakewell and Benjamin Page, from Derby, England. The firm they established was known first as Bakewell & Company and eventually as Bakewell & Page. The quality of glass was excellent, and it greatly resembled imported glass of the day. The chief method of decoration was cutting—an innovation in the American glass industry (see Color Plate D). Characteristic patterns of the earliest productions of the company are rayed circles, floral motifs, circles of joined fans, sunbursts, and strawberries (see Ill. 67).

Bakewell & Page had the longest life of any nineteenth century American glasshouse—from 1808 until 1882. The output of the early period included every variety of tableware, plus chandeliers and lamps. Some later patterns which the firm incorporated were Prism, Thistle, Argus, Cherry, Flute, and Heart. This company was an extremely successful one and it attracted nationwide attention. In 1817 President Monroe ordered a large service engraved with the arms of the United States. The Franklin Institute in Philadelphia, one of America's first science societies, awarded prizes to the company in 1824 and 1825 for the superior quality of its glass.

Because of the problems involved in attributing cut glass, it is difficult to assign pieces to the Bakewell factory unless they have a documented history. Inspired by the great success of this glasshouse, numerous others began to spring up in the Pittsburgh area. Much of this glass was mold-blown and is found cut and undecorated. While most of it was clear, it was sometimes made in blue, amethyst, and emerald green. Although glass from the Pittsburgh area has its own particular characteristics and patterns, it is difficult to attribute it to a specific maker.

The next major step in flint glass manufacturing took place in the Boston area. Another Englishman, Thomas Cains, who had been trained as a glassmaker in Bristol, came to Boston in 1811. He learned of the success of the Pittsburgh enterprises, rented space from an existing glasshouse in South Boston, and began to make flint glass. A group of Cains' workmen left his factory in 1814 to establish a glasshouse in Cambridge which became known as the New England Glass Company.

Since the majority of workmen for this factory also came from England and Ireland, it is only natural that the tradition of these countries should dominate the design of the glass. Cutting was emphasized and a large variety of tableware as well as lamps and chemical ware was produced. It is difficult to attribute the products of these factories also unless they have documented histories.

Blown molded pieces were being made at the Cambridge factory as early as 1820. One of the most familiar forms was the salt dish which was advertised in both an octagonal and fan-end shape (see Ill. 68). These salts were blown into single molds that were the full size of the piece and the edges of the finished product were ground with a cutting machine. The desired effect was that of cut glass. This was the most primitive method of blowing into molds and the end products have a considerable clumsiness.

A new method was perfected by 1830 which allowed more grace and refinement in blown molded pieces. This was blowing a thin glass into a hinged mold which could easily be opened, and then working it with tools. Since the molds generally had three sections, this type of glass became known as blown three-mold glass. Three faint ridges or seams may be detected on pieces of this type. Whether the mold had less or more than three parts, all glass of this type is called blown three-mold. A note of caution is pertinent

114

here. Collectors should be certain that a piece of glass on which seams are detectable has been blown; seams on pressed glass have no relevance to this discussion.

The earliest designs of blown three-mold glass were of a geometric nature—waffles, sunbursts, diapered patterns—and were derivative of cut-glass patterns. Later, cornucopias, bulls'-eyes, and Gothic arches all became a part of the design repertory—thus following the popular revival design trends of the day. This glass was pretty much limited to table articles, and a single mold would often provide the basis for the design of a tumbler, decanter, and inkwell.

Blown three-mold glass was generally clear but it is sometimes found in amethyst, blue, green, purple, or yellow. Most of the surviving examples have been attributed to three glasshouses of New England, although some were made at Pittsburgh and other places in the Midwest. The factory at Keene, New Hampshire, was famous for its decanters and inkwells (see Ill. 69).

Deming Jarves (1790-1861), who was the first manager of the Cambridge firm, founded his own Boston and Sandwich Glass Company on Cape Cod in 1825. Boston and Sandwich, probably the most famous name in nineteenth century glassmaking, produced not only blown and blown molded wares, but also pressed wares, which will be discussed later. The blown pieces were often of a classic simplicity and were made of glass of exquisite colors (see Ill. 66). A great variety of blown three-mold patterns was executed here, varying from the simplest geometric patterns to many variations on the Baroque and other revival patterns.

After Jarves's departure from Cambridge, another Englishman, Thomas Leighton, took his place. Various members of the family remained in charge of the factory until 1874, and they were noted for the fine pieces of blown glass which they produced. The Leightons were especially well known for the introduction

76 Paperweight, blown clear glass with infused colored rods, c. 1875. Attributed to the Clyde Glass Works (Clyde, New York) which was operated by Southwick, Reed & Co. Paperweights were produced in many colors and forms; this example is attributed to a country glasshouse from which only a few other documented examples survive.
The Brooklyn Museum.

77 Match holder, blown Peachblow glass, c. 1880. New England Glass Company. This example, in the shape of a tricorner hat, has the rich coloring so characteristic of Peachblow.
The Brooklyn Museum.

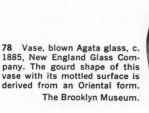

78 Vase, blown Agata glass, c. 1885, New England Glass Company. The gourd shape of this vase with its mottled surface is derived from an Oriental form.
The Brooklyn Museum.

79 Bowl, blown Amberina glass, c. 1885; probably Mount Washington Glass Company (New Bedford, Massachusetts). The coloring of this piece varies from a very deep red at the bottom to a vibrant yellow at the rim; this is the characteristic color of Amberina.
The Brooklyn Museum.

80 Vase, blown iridescent glass, c. 1900, signed "L. C. Tiffany Favrile." The tulip shape of this vase is an excellent example of the infusion of nature directly into Tiffany's glass; it is an eloquent statement of *Art Nouveau*.
The Brooklyn Museum.

of vivid colors, with the ruby glass of the mid-century ranking as foremost in popularity.

Running concurrently with the large flint glasshouses, whose products were European in their inspiration, were country glass-houses that produced bottle and window glass. It was in these factories that bottles and flasks were made on which can be traced the history of the United States. Whether it was a celebration honoring a national figure, or the opening of a new railroad, all events were recorded on the historical flasks. These centers of manufacture were located in the Midwest and in rural areas of the East, with the factories near Saratoga, New York, and Millville, New Jersey, ranking high in importance. With these wares the glass industry took on an American character and new urban glasshouses began to spring up in Brooklyn, Philadelphia, and other cities—more than one hundred in all between 1820 and 1840.

Pressed Glass. The pressing of glass had been practiced in the early 1820's but simple knobs were the only product. The first shallow piece, a salt, was pressed in 1826 at the Cambridge factory. Deming Jarves had been pressing cup plates and other shallow vessels at Sandwich. However, in 1827 he perfected a mold and hand-operated machine and produced a tumbler—a great revolution in glassmaking. The prospect of mechanization so frightened the workmen at Sandwich that they threatened Jarves's life. A drawing of this first pressed-glass tumbler still survives which reveals that it carried a simple bull's-eye pattern between two pillars. All of the earliest pressed wares were of a simple nature, with salts continuing to be an important form. One of the most universal was the rectangular salt decorated with a basket of flowers in raised detail (see Ill. 71).

The perfection of this machine led to the production of "lacy glass," so-called because of the elaborate background which often resembles lace. Most pieces of this type were designed so that the stippled background covered the entire piece. The patterns were borrowed directly from the idiom of Empire design; cornucopias, swags, lyres, patriotic symbols, acanthus leaves and similar motifs make up the vocabulary. As other revival styles became popular they were also reflected in glass, so it is not surprising that Gothic arches and other devices began to be seen in the 1830's and 1840's. By this time, lacy glass was being pressed in all forms. Salts were produced in an endless variety of shapes and designs, as were cup plates, the small plate used to hold a handleless cup. The ware was usually clear, but examples also survive in amethyst, light blue, peacock blue, canary yellow, or green.

Another type of pressed glass also began to be popular during the 1830's. This attempted to imitate the designs and appearance of cut-glass tableware. It was called "pattern glass" because it was produced in large sets which provided virtually everything for the table. The first American-made goblets were of this type, for this was a form that was never made in lacy glass. At first the designs were quite simple and borrowed diamond points, prisms, and flutes from cut glass. The patterns became more complex, and eventually embraced circles, ovals, and generally elliptical patterns (see Ill. 72). During the Civil War period, naturalistic details such as bellflowers, ivy, and grapes began to be used against a ribbed background. The glass of this type, as well as of the earlier patterns, is heavy, bell-like when struck, and generally of a high quality.

A soda-lime base, however, was eventually to be used in the manufacture of pattern glass. William Leighton (a member of the family previously mentioned in connection with the Cambridge factory) developed a formula in the 1860's which perfectly fitted soda-lime glass for pressing. While most of the midwestern factories chose to use this new formula, the New England factories

118

stuck to the manufacture of flint glass. Because the soda-lime glass was of inferior quality, more elaborate designs were developed which covered the entire surface of the piece, and thus obscured the imperfections. The designs were of a naturalistic and sentimental quality and provide an excellent mirror of Victorian taste (see Ill. 73). This glass continued to be produced throughout the second half of the century. It was made in enormous quantities and was very inexpensive at the time.

Among the most successful wares of the 1876 period were the frosted and clear patterns. The Gillinder family of Philadelphia treated glass surfaces with an acid finish; this was known as frosted or camphor glass. The Ribbon, Westward Ho, and Lion were familiar patterns of this type (see Ill. 74). During the last twenty-five years of the century the patterns had become so complex and so numerous that it would be impossible to treat them here. Exhaustive check lists of this glass have already been compiled and the reader is invited to consult the Bibliography for a list of such works.

Art Glass. Around the middle of the century, blown glass came into vogue and continued to rise in popularity until the end of the century. Victorian taste demanded a certain amount of elaboration as well as a feeling of massive solidity, and this could all be achieved only in blown glass. The blown glass wares from the second half of the century are generally referred to as "art glass" because of the elaborate technical problems which were involved in making them.

The New England Glass Company at Cambridge took the lead over all other factories in the production of art glass. One of the most popular wares made there in the early 1850's was Bohemian glass, which was named for the elaborately engraved wares imported from Bohemia, Germany, and Austria. The finest flint base material was used; casings of colored glass were applied over clear glass and designs were cut and engraved on the surface so that the underlying colors showed through. Sometimes as many as four layers of different color were applied so that the effect was spectacular when the glass was cut. This application of one layer over another is responsible for the name "overlay" which is often applied to this glass.

The earliest engravings on overlay glass were heavy and of a naturalistic nature. Later, about 1860, the designs became light and airy, with vintage patterns predominating. One of the chief engravers of this type of glass for the Cambridge factory was Louis Vaupel. His design and execution of patterns rank with the best that was being done in Europe at the time (see Ill. 75).

One of the constant themes of Victorian taste was a desire for novelty and few fields offered such unlimited opportunities for this as glassmaking. Paperweights were one of the most popular novelty items. There is a strong relationship between French and American paperweights of the day because of the migration of such glassmakers as Francois Pierre and Nicholas Lutz from that country to this.

Probably the most popular paperweight was the type called "millefiori." To create one of these objects of mysterious beauty, a gather of molten glass was first placed into a ball-shaped mold. Then colored glass rods, previously prepared, were heated and arranged in the desired pattern on the bottom of the mold of molten glass. Another gather of molten clear glass was placed over this and the entire object was removed from the mold. The only thing that remained to be done was polishing.

Some paperweights contained flowers, fruit, human figures, and a great variety of other decorative devices. Sometimes they were actually made in the shape of fruits. Among the most handsome were the weights that contained sulfide busts of national heroes.

Paperweights were universally produced throughout the second half of the century, sometimes in obscure glasshouses from which came few other documentable objects (see Ill. 76).

Another novelty that became very popular at mid-century was silvered glass. This attempted to imitate silver although no one would ever be taken in by it. The glass was blown double, and the interior was painted with a solution of silver nitrate. In general, this glass is not pleasing because the forms were poorly conceived and the silver nitrate was often applied in a shoddy manner. Sometimes these pieces were further decorated with etched vintage patterns. Today, this type of glass is known as mercury glass.

It was about the time of the Philadelphia Centennial Exhibition of 1876 that a major revolution began to take place in American glassmaking. The Oriental porcelains exhibited there had a great impact and created a desire to re-create the delicate coloring and decoration of these pieces in glass. It was discovered that through reheating a piece of colored glass, a great number of shadings of the original color could be produced. The two basic types of glass that were produced by this method were Peachblow and Amberina.

"Peachblow" was derived from the term "peach-bloom," which is used in describing a certain type of delicate Chinese porcelain. In the 1880's, J. P. Morgan created a nationwide sensation by paying an enormous price for a peach-bloom vase for his collection. A reproduction of this vase was made in glass with a glass base, rather than the teakwood of the original. There were two major types and centers of production of Peachblow, as the glass was called. That produced by Hobbs, Brockunier Company at Wheeling, West Virginia, shades from a light yellow to red to white, while that made at the New England Glass Company (Cambridge) ranges from opaque white to deep rose (see Ill. 77). Often these pieces were given a dull finish through the use of acids. Closely related to Peachblow was Agata, a glass also made at the Cambridge factory, whose surface was mottled through an acid treatment. Often these pieces were executed in Oriental shapes (see Ill. 78).

Amberina was a transparent flint glass, in contrast to the opaque Peachblow. It shaded in color from amber to deep red. Cambridge was a major center for the manufacture of Amberina as was the Mount Washington Glass Company at New Bedford, Massachusetts (see Ill. 79). The latter factory was well known for Burmese, a glass related to Amberina, which had a dull finish, shaded from yellow to pink, and sometimes had enameled decorations.

From 1885 until 1900 every variety of experiment was attempted with glass. Mica was infused into the glass to give it a sparkling quality, and rare metals were combined with the basic ingredients to produce varieties of color and quality. There was a great vogue for applied decoration on the surface of a piece. Often the form of a vase or basket was obscured by the ponderous decoration that was added to it. All of the hideosities of eclectic revivalism found their way into glass by the end of the century.

Louis Comfort Tiffany. A return to the concept that the fluid nature of glass should dominate the design is to be observed in the works of Louis Comfort Tiffany (1848-1933), whose name surely must rank as one of the greatest in the history of American glassmaking. Although he had been trained as a painter, Tiffany began to experiment with glassmaking in the 1870's. He established furnaces at Corona on Long Island and began to produce glass of vibrant colors for stained windows. Eventually, his attention turned to the iridescent coloring of ancient glass and he developed a method which captured this quality. Tiffany produced glass of every type—stained glass, tableware, and a great variety of ornamental and art wares (see Ill. 80).

It was the spirit of *Art Nouveau* that Tiffany captured so well in his glass. In an attempt to escape from the eclectic revivalism that was so rampant, he turned to nature and exquisitely reproduced it in his glass. The sweeping lines of these pieces were the boldest statement of *Art Nouveau* produced in America. At the century's end, Tiffany was flourishing and his influence has been felt on glass and design ever since.

Many of Tiffany's pieces were marked—sometimes with "L.C.T." and at other times with the full signature or a combination of initials and the last name. On the earlier pieces a gummed label was often attached, but eventually the signature was etched into the glass. The word "favrile" is often found with the signature; this meant that the piece was hand-made and is derived from the Latin for blacksmith.

Collecting Glass. Probably no collectible offers as many pitfalls as nineteenth century American glass. It has been actively collected for many years and now commands high prices. In addition, the popularity of pattern and other table glass has made it a standard reproduction item. Since some of these reproductions are made from the original molds, it is extremely difficult to distinguish them from the nineteenth century wares. When old molds were not available, new ones were made from old pieces and some of these reproductions are also very deceptive.

The intrinsic nature of glass makes it difficult to detect age. Sometimes the bottom of a piece will show signs of wear, but even this is not a definite clue as unscrupulous dealers have sometimes ground the bottoms of new pieces to achieve this effect. And of course, glass is rarely marked in any way; the two standard methods are etching the signature or having some statement pressed into the piece itself. Both of these methods can unfortunately be faked.

In the last fifteen years, art glass has also become very popular and is eagerly sought. Pieces by Tiffany have recently begun to command astronomical prices, as do other types that show the influence of *Art Nouveau*. With art glass and pattern glass tremendously popular, only the blown flint glass of the early part of the century remains. Surprisingly, bargains can still be found if one looks long and hard.

The best advice to a novice is to study a good museum glass collection. Learn to recognize the characteristics of each type and the execution of details. Of course, a visit to a reputable glass dealer should follow, so that feel may be determined and authentic signs of age can be studied. Numerous specialized books that deal with American glass are included in the Bibliography.

Lighting Devices

THE STUDY of lighting and its development is especially revealing to anyone interested in the decorative arts of any period because it combines a picture of changes in taste and style with a survey of advances in science and technology. Since men have generally wished to continue their daytime activities after dark, and because some method of artificial illumination is required for this, it would seem to follow that considerable thought and energy have always been directed toward improving lighting. This is not the case, however, for certain basic forms of lighting persisted for thousands of years, or until the end of the eighteenth century. It was only then that scientific minds began seriously to consider the problem and lay the foundations for the many lighting improvements we know today.

Candlesticks and Primitive Lamps. From earliest times a small open reservoir was filled with animal or vegetable fat and a wick of some combustible material was placed in it. When the wick was ignited, it burned with a feeble and odorous flame. This simple lamp, with countless variations, persisted into the nineteenth century in rural parts of the United States. It was often called a "betty" or "phoebe" lamp. Closely related to these crude lamps was the rushlight, which was made by dipping the pith of the soft rush in melted fat. After the fuel was absorbed by the rush it was put into an iron clamp, and one end of it was lighted.

The candle is another form that has survived since antiquity. Its basic principle, a refinement of the rushlight, is to surround a piece of wicking with a solid combustible material, usually beeswax, tallow or some vegetable substance. This is achieved by dipping the wick successively into the molten material or by molding the material around the wick. It is, of course, necessary to have some holder to support the candle. Thus the candlestick, with its relatives the candelabra and the chandelier, came into being.

The simple candlestick has a base, shaft, candle-cup or socket, and sometimes a removable member used to catch the dripping wax, called a *bobêche*. The candlestick has always closely reflected changes of taste, and the nineteenth century was certainly no exception. All of the revival styles are shown in this medium as completely as in furniture (see Ill. 26).

During the first forty years of the century, French taste was the dominant influence on American design, and the drawings of Percier and Fontaine included many designs for candelabra which were executed in ormolu (gilded bronze). Their book contains designs for *flambeaux, candelabres, appliques, bras de lumière, lustres,* and *lanternes.* The designs of these fixtures incorporate such Classical and antique devices as the sphinx, eagle and acanthus leaf in profusion. Many of these designs were executed by the Parisian firm of Thomière.

It is important to mention French Empire candlesticks, for a new phenomenon in lighting, one that is commonly accepted in the twentieth century, was beginning at that time—the introduction of lampshades. A large circular shade was placed at the top of a candelabrum with a key for adjusting its height. The shades were made of tin, brass, copper, or silver, and were often elaborately decorated with Empire devices. Shades were more commonly used on candelabra than on oil lamps. These shaded candelabra were called *bouillottes,* for they were often placed in the center of a table

126

1 *Bouillotte* candelabrum of brass with painted tin shade, the base inscribed: "Baker, Arnold & Company." This candelabrum, which closely follows French prototypes, was made in Philadelphia, c. 1804-1814.

The Henry Francis du Pont Winterthur Museum.

82 Double Argand lamp of bronze, bearing inscribed plate: "B. Gardiner, New York." Gardiner was active as a bronze-caster and lampmaker between 1827 and 1845.

Author's collection.

83 Single brass candlestick in the Empire style. The shape and fine-cut decoration place this candlestick in the period c. 1825.

Sleepy Hollow Restorations.

84 Pair of ormolu candlesticks with cut-glass prisms in a combination of the Gothic and Rococo revival styles. Such candlesticks were often called *girandoles*.

Sleepy Hollow Restorations, Gift of Mrs. Giles Whiting.

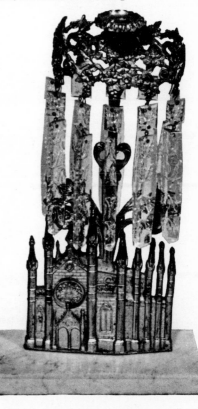

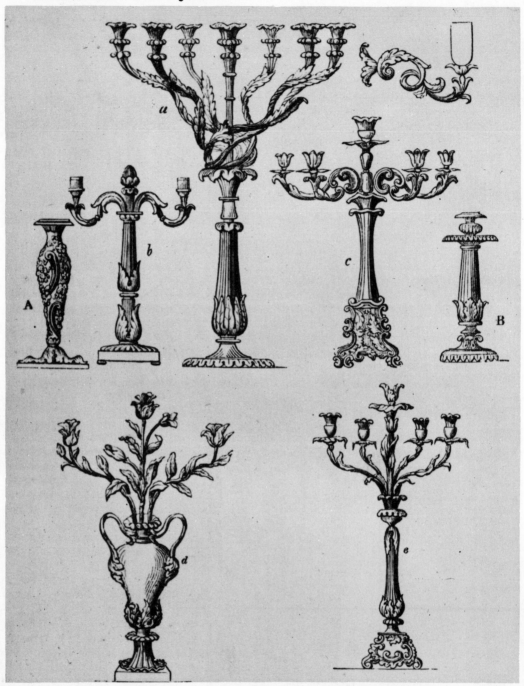

Fig. 26 Engraving from Webster's *Encyclopaedia* (1844) which shows candlesticks and candelabra in the Rococo and Classical styles.

used for this popular French card game. Some fine examples were made in America, especially by Baker, Arnold & Company, of Philadelphia (see Ill. 81).

The remainder of the century saw the candlestick influenced by all the revival styles. Since this subject has been previously treated, it should suffice to mention this development and to show several examples (see Ills. 83 & 84).

Lamps. It was in the design and development of lamps that significant progress was made during the nineteenth century. The first important technological step toward the improvement of lighting was made during the last quarter of the eighteenth century. In 1783, a Swiss chemist named Ami Argand developed a lamp constructed on principles of scientific combustion. This lamp embodied a hollow tube, open at both ends, which extended upward through the center of the burner. A cylindrical woven wick was fitted tightly around the tube and an outer cylinder was placed around this. Oil from the reservoir was fed into the side of the cylindrical chamber containing the wick. The hollow tube served to admit air to the center of the flame, thus increasing combustion and the amount of light as heat from the flame acted automatically to create a draft. The draft was further increased by the addition of a glass chimney. The reservoir of the Argand lamp was placed above the level of the flame so that gravity would cause the oil to flow to the burner as it was needed (Fig. 27). The principle of the Argand burner was incorporated into fixtures with varying numbers of arms and uses. Some of these were hanging lamps, some wall brackets, and others were of the table variety (Fig. 28). The Argand-type lamp persisted as a standard form until the middle of the century.

It is interesting to note that two of the most noted American manufacturers of Argand lamps began their careers as silver-

Fig. 27 Engraving from Webster's *Encyclopaedia* (1844), showing the construction of the Argand burner.

Fig. 28 Four hanging lanterns, from Webster's *Encyclopaedia* (1844), which incorporate single-wick and Argand lamps.

130

smiths and turned their energies to bronze-lamp casting. One of these was Baldwin Gardiner, who worked as a silversmith in Boston before 1812, moved to Philadelphia and founded the bronze-casting firm of Fletcher and Gardiner, then eventually went to New York, where he managed his own concern between 1827 and 1845. The quality of his lamps was excellent and they were often designed in a transitional phase between Classical and Rococo in a contrasting bronze and gilt bronze. Many of his lamps bear a bronze label engraved "B. Gardiner, New York" (see Ill. 82).

Christian Cornelius of Philadelphia was the other manufacturer of fine lamps. He also worked as a silversmith before 1812, and then founded a firm which went through the successive names of C. Cornelius & Son, Cornelius & Co., and finally Cornelius & Baker. They were the largest lamp manufacturers and ornamental founders in the United States by 1845. The renown and importance of this company were to last through the end of the century.

As in many fields of invention, after the initial step toward the improvement of lighting had been made by Argand, a number of other developments quickly followed. In 1787, John Miles of Birmingham, England, patented his agitable burner, a simple device that was in no sense a scientific advance. The lamp was merely a container with a hole at the top into which a burner with one or more wick tubes could be screwed or tightly fitted. The container was filled with whale oil which was soaked up by the vertical wicks through capillary action.

Although the whaling industry was well established when Miles developed his burner, the popularity of these whale oil lamps, as they were called, certainly contributed to the expansion of the industry after 1800. By 1830, the whale oil lamp was a standard fixture in the average home. The glass industries at Cambridge, Sandwich, and Pittsburgh produced these lamps in great quantity, as did local pewterers and tinsmiths (see Ill. 88).

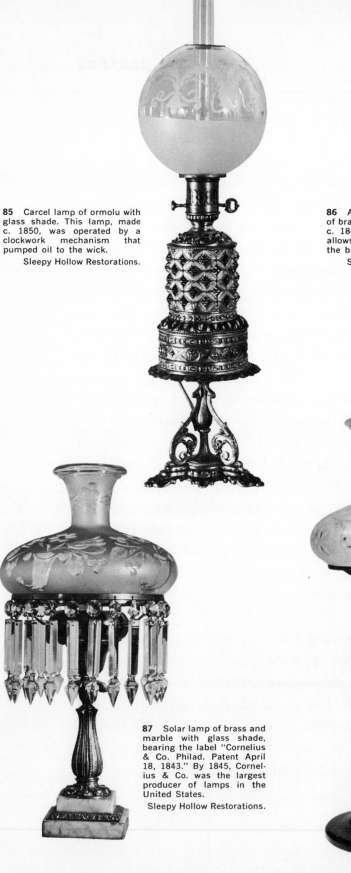

85 Carcel lamp of ormolu with glass shade. This lamp, made c. 1850, was operated by a clockwork mechanism that pumped oil to the wick.

Sleepy Hollow Restorations.

86 Astral, or sinumbra, lamp of brass with glass shade, made c. 1840. The circular reservoir allows light to shine below on the base.

Sleepy Hollow Restorations.

87 Solar lamp of brass and marble with glass shade, bearing the label "Cornelius & Co. Philad. Patent April 18, 1843." By 1845, Cornelius & Co. was the largest producer of lamps in the United States.

Sleepy Hollow Restorations.

88 Whale-oil lamp with deep amethyst glass base and frosted and cut shade; marked "N.E. Glass Co. Boston." The double whale-oil burner is concealed behind the shade in this example, which dates c. 1830-1855.

The Henry Francis du Pont Winterthur Museum.

In 1830, an American, Isaiah Jennings, patented a new fuel which he called his "burning fluid." This fuel contained alcohol and spirits of turpentine in a proportion of eight to one. The burner used with this mixture closely resembled that of the whale oil lamp, except that the two wick tubes slanted away from each other because of the high inflammability of the fluid.

In 1830, the year the fuel was patented, the Franklin Institute *Journal* commented that Jennings' burning fluid was to be highly recommended because of the clearness and brilliance of its light, and because it could be produced more cheaply than whale oil. However, by 1834, the *Journal* had revised its opinion. Camphene, as Jennings' burning fluid was eventually called, was discovered to be dangerous to use, and a number of fatal accidents occurred. Newspapers of the first half of the nineteenth century furnish ample evidence of explosions resulting from the use of camphene. Because of this, it was never a successful lamp fluid.

It was again the French who made an important improvement on the Argand lamp. This was the annular lamp, in which the oil reservoir was moved so that it fitted under the shade and was circular in shape. The fuel, which was a refined whale oil, ran from the reservoir through the two fuel tubes, and thence to the wick. The lamp still incorporated an Argand-type burner (Fig. 29).

In America during the 1830's and 1840's, this was the lamp most popularly used on elegant parlor tables, and it was called "astral." The term "sinumbra" (without shadow) is synonymous with astral as a name for this type of lamp. They were fitted with ground-glass shades resting on ring-shaped, or annular, reservoirs, which were designed to minimize the amount of shadow cast by the reservoir. They were made of brass, bronze, and sometimes of silver or pressed glass. Like the common lamps that burned in less important parts of the house, astral lamps utilized whale oil (see Ill. 86). Astral lamps continued to be popular until about 1850.

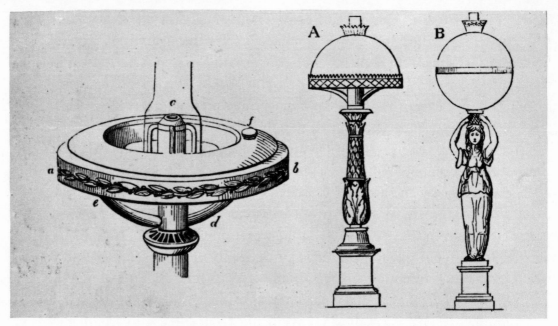

Fig. 29 The reservoir and burner of an astral, or sinumbra, lamp, from Webster's *Encyclopaedia* (1844).

Closely related to the astral was the solar lamp. This incorporated a modified Argand burner and was designed to burn lard. The reservoir was located directly beneath the flame, and an interior device shaded the flame so that it became a column of light. The burner was patented by Cornelius & Co. in 1843. The bases and shades of these lamps were often conceived in a mixture of the then popular revival styles. Solar lamps were economical and highly efficient; they were popular simultaneously with astral lamps in the 1840's and 1850's (see Ill. 87). Solar chandeliers were also popular, and enrichment with glass and bronze ornament added to their decorative effect (Fig. 30).

The Carcel or "mechanical" lamp was invented in France in 1800, but was never widely used in the United States until the middle of the century. The Argand burner was still utilized with the addition of an elaborate clockwork mechanism which controlled a pump that sent oil to the burner. The lamp used whale oil and burned with a bright intense light that was protected by a vertical chimney and round shade. These lamps were costly, and small numbers of them were made in the United States. They were generally conceived in a combination of Classical and Rococo revival detail (see Ill. 85).

Natural gas was one of the most revolutionary lighting sources utilized during the century. It is curious that although David Melville of Newport, Rhode Island, used gas for domestic lighting in 1806 and Rembrandt Peale used it in 1816 to illuminate his museum in Baltimore, it was not commonplace until after the Civil War. Unlike other lighting devices, the gas fixture had to be sta-

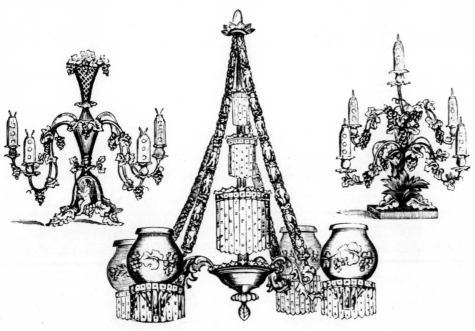

Fig. 30 Solar chandelier shown in an advertisement of R. H. Spalding, of Boston, in the *National Portrait Gallery* (1853).

tionary, and varied from single jets with little ornament to ponderous chandeliers which incorporated revival detail. Glass shades or globes were used to protect the burning gas jet from drafts. Cornelius & Co. exhibited two chandeliers at the Crystal Palace (1851), one of which was in the naturalistic Rococo idiom (Fig. 31). This firm was still flourishing near the end of the century, for it exhibited a chandelier at the Philadelphia Centennial. This enormous creation was conceived in a medieval manner

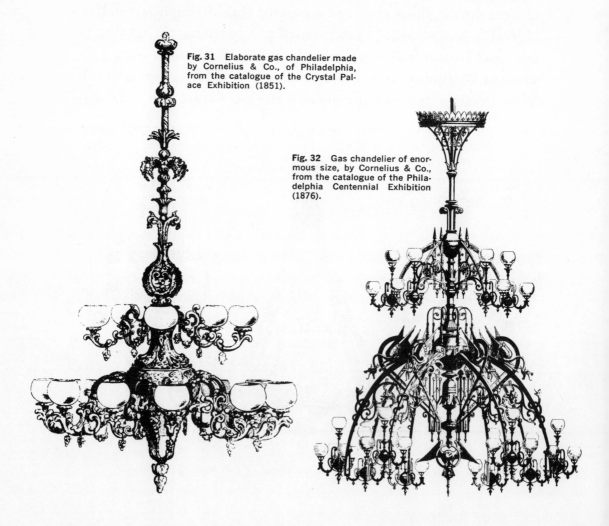

Fig. 31   Elaborate gas chandelier made by Cornelius & Co., of Philadelphia, from the catalogue of the Crystal Palace Exhibition (1851).

Fig. 32   Gas chandelier of enormous size, by Cornelius & Co., from the catalogue of the Philadelphia Centennial Exhibition (1876).

with Gothic detail and grotesque monsters. It well illustrates the overabundance of ornament crowded onto objects made for the international exhibitions (Fig. 32).

Kerosene was the one burning fluid that had replaced all others in importance by the end of the century. It was known as early as 1824, when Abraham Gesner of Williamsburg, New York, patented his "new liquid hydrocarbon, which I denominate kerosene." However, the fuel was never cheap enough to attain great popularity until the oil fields of Pennsylvania were opened about 1859. The excellence of kerosene, or "coal oil," as it was often called, was so immediately realized that by 1866 the United States boasted 194 kerosene distilleries, with an annual output of twenty-eight million gallons.

The exact steps by which the kerosene burner evolved have not as yet been traced. The features that gave the kerosene lamp such prominence were a flat wick, a spur that could raise or lower the wick, and a dome-shaped contrivance that covered the wick and protected it. This dome-shaped draft deflector was generally fitted with prongs which held secure a cylindrical glass chimney. Glass shades, sometimes painted, were used to further filter the light. By the last quarter of the century, shades of paper and cloth were commonly in use.

The kerosene lamp was made from glass, pottery, brass, bronze, and any number of metallic alloys. The shapes and styles were almost always derived from historical ornaments, often badly mixed in context (Fig. 33). Chandeliers, wall brackets, standing adjustable "piano" lamps, and every variety of table model were created. Art glass was used to make many varieties of miniature and regular-sized table lamps. By the end of the century, "china lamps" were especially popular, their bases and shades painted with bright flowers or other detail (Fig. 34). The "student lamp" was another innovation of the end of the century.

Gravitational flow was utilized in this lamp as it had been in the Argand type. The light source and shade could be swung around so that it was a highly practical reading lamp (Fig. 35). There is no better source than the Sears, Roebuck catalogues to show popular taste in lighting during the last years of the century.

Collecting Lighting Devices. The development of lighting has been of great interest to collectors for many years—so much so that clubs have been formed dedicated to the study of lighting. Such a developmental collection is not decorative, however, and the field of lamps that can be converted to electricity has not received the attention it deserves.

Marvelous bargains are still to be found in the lamps of the first half of the century—especially of the Argand and astral types. Many of these are beautifully made and they often bear their makers' labels. They are especially handsome when they are used in combination with other furnishings of the period.

Lighting devices from the last quarter of the century offer the collector many problems. Often these were mass-produced of cheap materials and are so eclectic in design that all form is lacking. These lamps have more value as curios than as truly collectible objects.

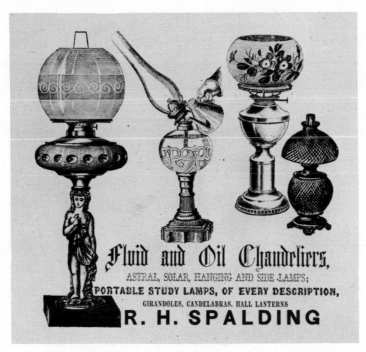

Fig. 33 Advertisement of R. H. Spalding, of Boston, showing four different styles of kerosene lamps, c. 1865.

Fig. 34 China parlor lamp which burned kerosene, from the Sears, Roebuck *Catalogue* (1900).

Fig. 35 Brass student lamp with glass shade, from the Sears, Roebuck *Catalogue* (1900).

139

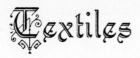

Textiles

Homespun **Textiles.** In 1800, textiles were being manufactured in the home in much the same manner as they had been almost two centuries earlier when the first settlers came to America. The raising of flax for linen and sheep for wool was one of the earliest necessities imposed upon the New England settlers, but by the turn of the nineteenth century cotton was becoming more commonly utilized in domestic textile making.

Spinning and weaving have generally been regarded as work closely associated with the home and women. However, much documentary evidence survives to show that men and boys also practiced these crafts in the nineteenth century American home. The raw material was first treated with a set of cards, or combs, with wooden backs and metal teeth; this was to remove any impurities and to break the fibers apart. After the carding operation was completed, a spinning wheel was used to weave the fibers into threads. Then the threads were sometimes dyed with whatever colors were available to the housewife. The final process was the weaving of the threads on a loom, with the eventual production of a piece of cloth. Looms varied in size; tapes used for trimming could be made on a simple hand loom, while large pieces of goods were usually made on hand- and foot-operated mechanisms. The pattern and colors combined in a piece of cloth depended upon the imagination and skill of the artisan. Stripes, plaids and checks

140

89 Picture of a parrot and flowers, made of wool and raised Berlin work, c. 1860. The elaborateness of this type of work is well shown here.

Henry Ford Museum.

90 Framed picture of wool, paper, wire, and Berlin work, c. 1870. The picture frame gives the effect of a shadow box.

Henry Ford Museum.

91 Pincushion decorated with beadwork in elaborate floral patterns, c. 1880.

Henry Ford Museum.

92 Woven woolen coverlet of elaborate pattern, c. 1845. Both the Rococo and the Classical revivals contributed to the design of this coverlet.

Henry Ford Museum.

93 Handbag made of needlepoint, c. 1850. The fielded rosettes are borrowed from Classical ornament.

Henry Ford Museum.

were commonly used as patterns in these homemade fabrics.

To relieve the monotony of household chores, a phenomenon known as the "bee" evolved. This was a gathering of women for the express purpose of helping one another with some task while they exchanged news and ideas. Often a spinning and weaving bee took the form of a contest to see who could outdo all the others in the practice of her craft. There are numerous accounts of the fierce battles which raged among the participants in these contests. Quilting was another form of cooperative endeavor; each woman made a square or other geometric form of patchwork, which was then combined into the overall design.

One of the home crafts which persisted well into the nineteenth century was the weaving of coverlets made of wool over white cotton or linen coverlets. These were often woven in two contrasting colors, although examples in more colors do survive. These coverlets were most elaborate during the period from about 1825 to about 1850. As might be expected, the designs were often taken from one of the revival styles, with patriotic emblems being favored among these. The designer or weaver often proudly wove her name and the date into the border of the coverlet (see Ill. 92).

Handwork and Fancy Work. Throughout the century, many forms of needlework were considered a proper and genteel pastime for women. A young lady's education was not considered complete until she had mastered at least some of these arts and knew how to make small decorative pieces of wearing apparel as well as other useful household objects.

Embroidery, the use of the needle for purely decorative purposes, was certainly the most popular of these pastimes; it consists of stitching with a needle and thread a design drawn on a

94 Printed cotton handkerchief, stamped "Gray and Todd," which was made in Philadelphia, c. 1817. Masonic symbols form the complete decoration for this piece.

Mrs. Benjamin Ginsburg.

95 Printed cotton textile depicting "Constitution and Laws," which is stamped "Boston Chemical Printing Company." This firm is thought to have been active c. 1830.

Miss Elinor Merrell.

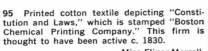

96 Printed cotton textile, "Harrison and Reform," made c. 1830. The patriotic elements are printed against a drab background.

Miss Elinor Merrell.

piece of fabric. The stitches are of many types and thread of various kinds can be used. There are basically two kinds of embroidery: crewel-work, which is executed with a loosely twisted worsted yarn generally in a flowing pattern, and needlepoint, which is produced by sewing on canvas with woolen yarn. A thick stitch in needlepoint is called a "cross stitch," while "tent stitch" is used to denote a single stitch carried diagonally over a thread of canvas. In either instance, the design is frequently geometric (see Ill. 93).

One highly decorative form of needlework was called "stuffed work," or "trapunto." To achieve a three-dimensional effect, a layer of fine cotton cloth was placed over a piece of coarser material. This was quilted together in a pattern that was generally floral. Thread was pushed through tiny holes to give the piece a padded appearance. Some of the designs were very elaborate, and considerable mastery of needlecraft was necessary to make a fine piece of stuffed work.

Candle-wicking was another related form. Several threads were used at once and worked over a rod in knotted form. The knots could be left as loops or they could be cut to give a tufted appearance. An elaborate variant of this was raised Berlin work, in which a free-standing figure was created in front of a simple needlepoint background. The body of the design was stuffed with cotton and embroidered-over with wool yarn. The yarn ends were trimmed so that they gave a highly naturalistic effect (see Ill. 89).

Work with wool yarn probably reached its zenith in the elaborate pictures that were made around the middle of the century. These were intended to be exhibited in frames under glass, and the designers' desires for originality often knew no bounds. Compositions varied from mourning pictures to landscapes and decorative floral arrangements. In addition to woolwork, these pictures sometimes incorporated objects made of paper, wax, wire, and human or animal hair. The elaborateness of some indicates that months must have been involved in their creation (see Ill. 90).

Beadwork was an allied art. Boxes of small glass beads in all colors were purchased and the beads were strung together and sewn onto a surface in a profusion of patterns. Sometimes this work was of a free-form nature applied to a textile while in other instances the beads were applied to the entire surface with a stitch which caused the product to resemble needlepoint (see Ill. 91).

Lacemaking was also a needlecraft that was practiced to a limited extent in nineteenth century America. However, the domestic product could never compete with the intricacy of European lace, so this remained one of the standard luxury imports throughout the century.

Mechanization and Textile Production. A number of factors connected with the Industrial Revolution combined to take the textile industry out of the home and place it in the factory. By the end of the eighteenth century a carding mill had been perfected which completely eliminated the painstaking hand method of carding. Usually one person in a neighborhood would purchase one of these mills and people from the area would bring their wool to it; the mill owner would card it and charge the individual a small sum for the operation.

The development of the fulling and dyeing mill, or finishing mill, was the second significant development in the mechanization of the textile industry. Hand-woven cloth was sent here to be cleansed or fulled, to have a nap raised, to be sheared until the proper pile was achieved, and sometimes to be dyed. These mills were also operated on a neighborhood basis. The only home operation now left was the actual weaving, which took place between the carding and finishing.

145

98 Printed cotton banner of the "Cotton Centenary" of 1890. Shows Samuel Slater and the original Slater mill against a background of the American flag.

Miss Elinor Merrell.

97 Printed cotton textile with fielded panel of George Washington and justice and peace. This is a typical example of the type of designs which were being produced c. 1876.

Miss Elinor Merrell.

99 Printed cotton handkerchief, showing "Samuel Slater The Father of American Manufacturers," made in 1890. It bears the imprint "Engraved at James Provan & Sons, Prov. R.I."

Miss Elinor Merrell.

100 Printed cotton textile, showing the joys of honest labo[r] made c. 1895. The same drab background of the 1840's co[n]tinued to be used.

Miss Elinor Merre[ll]

More important inventions were developed in England during the eighteenth century which rapidly mechanized the textile industry there: A fly shuttle developed by John Kay (1733), a spinning machine patented in 1738, James Hargreaves' spinning jenny (1768), Richard Arkwright's patented carding machine (1775), and finally Edmond Cartwright's automatic loom (1785). However, these inventions were carefully guarded by the English and none of the secrets were allowed to be used in America.

It was an enterprising Englishman named Samuel Slater who made the first mechanized spinning jenny in America. He had worked for many years with one of Arkwright's partners in an English mill. Slater familiarized himself with the construction details of the jenny and was able to reconstruct one from memory. George Cabot opened the first successful textile manufactory at Beverly, Massachusetts, in 1787. Carding and spinning machines and looms were all constructed by men who had worked with them in England. The factory turned out muslins, velvets, dimity, and other goods until it burned in 1810.

A cotton mill was built at Providence, Rhode Island, by Samuel Slater for Moses Brown and William Almy. Slater acted as operating manager there until he opened his own mill in Pawtucket in 1799. By 1810 cotton mills had begun to spring up in a number of New England towns. The War of 1812 set back the textile industry, but in 1813 in Waltham, Massachusetts, the first factory was opened which utilized machines for every process in the manufacture of cotton cloth; Francis Cabot Lowell was the principal owner. Most of the workers in these early factories were children or young farm girls.

Hand printing of designs on cotton and linen was carried on in America early in the eighteenth century. Generally this was done with carved wooden blocks, and the designs were crude and indistinct. The first factory for printing cotton was established in

Philadelphia in 1774 by John Hewson with the assistance of Benjamin Franklin. Early printing factories also existed in New Haven and Boston. The most important single development to mechanize cotton printing was the engraved cylinder, which was patented by Mathias Baldwin. The Taunton Massachusetts Company was organized in 1823; three years later it was turning out from 1,500 to 2,000 pieces weekly which were printed by engraved rollers.

Unfortunately, little documentary evidence exists to aid in the identification of the types of fabrics the individual factories produced. A large handkerchief survives which was probably printed from a copper plate and is stamped by Gray and Todd, who were active in Philadelphia about 1817. The handkerchief is elaborately decorated with Masonic emblems, a popular device of the time (see Ill. 94). Slightly later in date is another printed handkerchief, probably about 1830, which bears the stamp of the Boston Chemical Printing Company. This handkerchief resembles one of the wood-block prints that have been found in schoolbooks of the period. The subject is "Constitution and Laws" and the concept highly patriotic. Of great interest is the wide border with its Classical-inspired foliage (see Ill. 95). Another example of the work of this factory, entitled "The Blackberry Girl," is owned by the Smithsonian Institution.

American printed cotton yard goods, or chintz as it is often called, is still more difficult to identify. English and French fabrics of the day certainly served as models, but the poor quality of the printing, the limited range of colors, and the patriotic subject matter all help to identify the native products. The Harrison and Reform print of 1830-1840 well demonstrates all of these points. The lack of printed detail is obvious, the predominant colors are brown and a dull green, and the log cabin, the barrel of hard cider, and the bust of Harrison are all patriotic symbols (see Ill. 96).

Of later date, but closely identified with the Harrison chintz, was one which portrayed Zachary Taylor on horseback; it dates 1846-1848.

Throughout the century further refinements were made in American power-driven textile machinery. By the third quarter of the century the United States was exporting printed cottons around the world. At the Philadelphia Centennial quantities of cottons of American manufacture were exhibited. Many of these were naturally of a historical type and pictures of the "Founding Fathers" found their way into textile design. The characteristic print of this type showed a small fielded oval with a patriotic bust enclosed, the ovals generally tied together with a naturalistic pattern. The Centennial print of Washington is a good example of this, the ovals bearing the first President's bust enclosed by leafy patterns and shields proclaiming justice and peace (see Ill. 97).

In 1890 a centenary of the cotton industry in America was celebrated; some of the best documented fabrics from the end of the century date from this occasion. A banner printed on white cotton in red and blue shows a bust of Samuel Slater, enclosed in an oval of oak leaves and acorns. A similar oval surrounds a picture of the original Slater Mill. The stars and stripes and color of the banner simulate the American flag (see Ill. 98). Another souvenir of the centenary is a handkerchief that shows Slater, "The Father of American Manufacturers," in the center with views of Pawtucket. An interesting addition to this piece is the printed line "Engraved at James Provan & Sons, Prov. R. I." (see Ill. 99). The chintzes of the end of the century continued to be printed in the same drab colors of the 1840's. A typical example shows the joys of honest labor; against a brown background are various scenes of labor and the laborers' home. These are surrounded by flowers and leaves in an end-of-the-century restatement of the Rococo revival.

Woolens and silks were also produced in the United States during the nineteenth century. However, because of an almost complete lack of evidence linking the names of factories to examples of their wares, it is an extremely difficult subject to discuss.

Collecting Textiles. American textiles have been popular with collectors for many years. However, as this brief essay indicates, there is still a great lack of knowledge about the types and patterns of fabrics produced by individual factories. Any nineteenth century textile that bears the name of an American printer is a collectible item and should be watched for. It must be remembered, however, that they come to light only rarely.

An area where the collector can still find superb examples often at reasonable cost, is that of fancy work. There is the added attraction that raised Berlin work and embroidered pictures and accessories are bright, colorful, and have a highly decorative effect. An interesting collection could be evolved based on the subject matter of these pieces, such as animals, birds, Biblical scenes, etc.

Most fabric collectors find it necessary to expand their interests to include fabrics that were used but not necessarily made, in America. Since textiles were imported in great quantities from England, France, and the Orient, a study of these provides an interesting background for the American-made examples.

Silver and Metalwork

Silversmithing. At the dawn of the nineteenth century, silversmithing was still practiced as a handcraft in the apprenticeship tradition. A young man was indentured to serve a master craftsman, usually at the age of fourteen, for a period of seven years. This assured the master trained help and a successor and allowed the apprentice to learn all the mysteries of the craft. Strict regulations bound both parties to the agreement, which was arranged when the period of apprenticeship began.

Learning the craft became a part of the daily life of the apprentice. He became familiar with the processes and tools that were used to fashion a piece of silver. The raw silver, sometimes in the form of outdated coins, was melted and refined to a true standard. Then it was poured into a mold or ingot, and eventually hammered into a sheet of the required thickness. From this sheet a circular piece was cut equal in size to the outside dimensions of the desired piece. Since silver becomes brittle when it cools, an annealing process was necessary throughout the entire operation. This was accomplished by means of a charcoal fire fanned by a hand bellows.

Eventually the body of the piece was formed through successive hammerings. Handles, spouts, and covers were made separately and applied to the piece. Small pieces such as hinge plates, finials, and thumbpieces were cast separately and applied. If relief deco-

151

101 Silver tea set, with impressed mark "T. Richards," who was active in New York City between 1815 and 1829. The simplified Classical style is shown well in these pieces.

Mrs. Giles Whiting.

102 Circular silver dish, with impressed mark "W. Thomson," who was working in New York City, c. 1810. The engraved initials "P V C" are those of Pierre Van Cortlandt II.

Mrs. Giles Whiting.

103 Silver mug impressed with the mark "Gale, Wood & Hughes," who were active in New York City through the 1830's. The engraving indicates that it was a presentation piece to one of the Schroeder family in 1841.

Mrs. Giles Whiting.

104 Five-piece silver tea and coffee service, bearing the mark "SamL Kirk," and dominical letter "F"; made in Baltimore, c. 1850. The repoussé patterns in the Rococo taste are well shown here.

The Brooklyn Museum.

ration was incorporated, chasing hammers and punches were employed. Gravers were used to incise any decorative details. Burnishing stones were finally used to hand polish the entire surface.

The application of the silversmith's mark was the final process in making a piece of silver. In Europe, guilds carefully controlled the hallmarking system, through which the silversmith's name, the place of manufacture, and date could be determined. No such system existed in America, although some silversmiths did use pseudohallmarks. More commonly found was the name of the silversmith against a stamped rectangle; by the early years of the nineteenth century, the place of manufacture was added to silver made in Philadelphia and New York.

"Plate" was the term most commonly applied to silver in the eighteenth and early nineteenth centuries. The English sterling standard was used at this time to regulate the quality of silver. This required that 925 out of 1,000 parts be pure silver, with the remaining 75 parts of copper, which hardened the silver. By 1840 the standard had been changed to 900 parts pure silver and 100 parts alloy. The term "Sterling" was not commonly in use until about 1860. The stamped terms "COIN" and "PURE SILVER" indicate that the piece is made of silver coins.

Style in Silver. The silver of 1800 was strongly under the influence of Classicism. The urn shape was most commonly employed for hollow pieces, and decoration took the form of beaded or reeded moldings and engraved bright-cut decoration. Many of the great silversmiths of the eighteenth century lived on into the nineteeth and their work was often in an earlier spirit. Leaders in this group were Benjamin Burt and Paul Revere in Boston, Ephraim Brasher, Samuel Johnson and Hugh Wishart in New York, Joseph Lownes, James Musgrave and Abraham Dubois in Philadelphia, and Louis Boehme in Baltimore. The Classical silver which came from the shops of these men had a strong English influence.

By 1825, French silver began to have an important influence in America. It was naturally the forms of the Empire style which silversmiths sought to imitate. Silver stock became heavier and pieces were conceived on a much larger scale. Geometric and round shapes were favored and antique Greek and Roman forms were copied. Die-cast ornament, which was conceived in the Greek key, laurel leaf and anthemion leaf, was applied to pieces of this type. An extremely interesting early piece of silver in this tradition is a plate made for a member of the Van Cortlandt family about 1810 by W. Thomson in New York City. The only decoration is a band of cast anthemion leaves which form a border around the outer rim of the plate (see Ill. 102).

The matching tea set became a very popular form during the late eighteenth century. The vogue became even greater in the early nineteenth, and the massive Empire style lent itself to expression in this form. Sometimes these were elaborately decorated with Classical motifs or conceived in an archaeologically correct shape. Perhaps even more interesting were the plain Empire tea sets which were often decorated with only raised panels. One of the New York masters of this type was Thomas Richards, who was active between 1815 and 1829 (see Ill. 101). Other important New York silversmiths of the period were William Forbes and George Gelston. At the same time, Obadiah Rich was working in Boston and Peter Bumm, Anthony Rasch, and Thomas Whartenby were active in Philadelphia.

The characteristics of Empire silver persisted into the 1840's although Romantic decoration was often used in combination with Classical devices. A misunderstood concept of Empire motifs was often seen in later pieces. A mug by Gale, Wood & Hughes, who were active in New York City in the 1830's, is a perfect example.

The applied borders no longer have the chaste Classical feeling, but begin to anticipate the Rococo revival (see Ill. 103).

Forks and knives were not widely produced in the United States until the 1850's, but the spoon was in common production during the first half of the century. Shapes changed from the coffin-end and rounded handles of 1800 to a plain "fiddle back" or down-curved spatulate handle. These were often stamped with a decorative device such as a sheaf of wheat, shell, or basket of flowers. In the mid 1830's the shape changed to an upturned spatulate handle.

The influence of the Rococo revival was to be observed quite early in silver. During the 1820's Samuel Kirk (working 1793-1872) of Baltimore began to introduce repoussé decoration in his silver forms. This was a raised decoration in an overall pattern which was generally naturalistic and Rococo in style. By the middle of the century Kirk was producing highly elaborate tea and coffee services in this style. These combined repoussé Rococo floral detail with highly sentimental scenes (see Ill. 104).

Style development in silver has always been conservative and the Classical and Rococo styles remained popular simultaneously. The Rococo revival was often given full interpretation by the jewelers who were becoming prominent during the 1850's. In New York, Tiffany & Co. and Ball, Thompkins & Black were especially prominent (see Ill. 105). In Philadelphia, J. E. Caldwell & Co. and Bailey & Co. were the fashionable stores (Fig. 36).

During the 1860's Renaissance ornaments began to be applied to silver forms. Most of these were borrowed from architectural detail. This style remained popular through the 1870's, when an increased elaboration of the form was to be observed (see Ill. 106). Dulled or matted finishes became popular at this time. The style of the 1890's was completely eclectic; borrowing from ancient Near Eastern civilizations and the Orient became quite common.

155

Fig. 36   Repoussé tea and coffee service, made by Bailey & Co. of Philadelphia, with the engraved date 1876; from the catalogue of the Philadelphia Centennial Exhibition.

Mechanization and Silver. The impact of mechanization on silver was so complete that the time-honored craft of 1800 was almost completely a factory process by 1870. Late in the eighteenth century a process was discovered in England by which thin coverings of silver could be applied over copper, a thermomechanical process that attached the silver by a kind of fusing. This was referred to as plated silverware or Sheffield plate, as much of it was produced in that part of England. Plating was done in the United States but the product was generally inferior to that of the English. Great quantities of this ware were imported by Americans.

It was a further refinement of plating, however, which completely revolutionized the manufacture of silver. This was electroplating, which allowed the process to be done completely by the

105 Three silver pieces with similar naturalistic Rococo detail, by three different New York City makers, all c. 1855. The coffee pot is marked: "Tiffany & Co. 550 Broadway,N.Y.," and the hot water kettle: "Ball, Thompkins & Black." Museum of the City of New York.

106 Silver tea and coffee service, bearing the mark: "Tiffany & Co. 550 Broadway,N.Y." and the engraved date "1869." Naturalism and Renaissance details are combined in these pieces.

Museum of the City of New York.

factory method. Derived from the chemical process of electrolysis, this method allowed the rapid and even plating of metals with silver. Although the process was known in England a few years earlier, it was not until 1847 that the first successful electroplated objects were offered for sale in the United States. The Rogers Brothers, William, Asa and Simeon, developed the process in Hartford, Connecticut.

Electroplating made possible the creation of large and overly elaborate objects which could never have been made of sterling silver. The revival forms were all represented in extraordinary objects made in this way. The exhibition catalogues from the last 25 years of the century demonstrate the low ebb of taste which was now possible in this medium (Fig. 37).

Pewter and Britannia Metal. Pewter is an alloy made of tin combined with parts of copper, brass, or lead. The component part of lead had to be carefully regulated, for a large percentage could induce poisoning. Pewtering as a craft is more correctly identified with the eighteenth than the nineteenth century. It was an ancient craft, practiced in much the same manner as silversmithing, with the pewterer affixing his touch mark to the finished product.

Pewter had been a kind of universal tableware during the eighteenth century. Plates, coffee and tea services, beakers, goblets, spoons and other utensils were fashioned from it. The pewter made in the early nineteenth century continued to be made in eighteenth century forms (see Ill. 108). By 1840 the individual pewterer had virtually disappeared. This was brought about by the ready availability of inexpensive china and pressed glass as well as the development of a new pewter-like alloy known as Britannia metal.

Britannia metal is the name applied to the alloy closely related to pewter. Tin is still the basic ingredient, with rich additions of copper and antimony. No lead was used, so the surface was brighter

107 Cast-iron dressing glass frame, with painted decoration, c. 1860. This type of mirror frame has often been called "Jenny Lind."
Sleepy Hollow Restorations.

108 Pewter beaker with touch mark: "T.D.&S.B.," by Thomas D. and Sherman Boardman, who were working in Hartford, Connecticut, between 1810 and 1830. This is a typical eighteenth century form which persisted into the nineteenth century.
Sleepy Hollow Restorations.

109 Teapot of Britannia metal, stamped: "Morey & Ober," who were working in Boston from 1852-1855. The handle has been painted black to simulate the wooden handle generally found on silver teapots.
Sleepy Hollow Restorations.

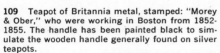

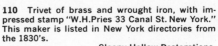

110 Trivet of brass and wrought iron, with impressed stamp "W.H.Pries 33 Canal St. New York." This maker is listed in New York directories from the 1830's.
Sleepy Hollow Restorations.

The Neptune Epergne: Meriden Britannia Co.

Fig. 37 Electroplated Britannia metal épergne, made by the Meriden (Conn.) Britannia Co.; from the catalogue of the Philadelphia Centennial Exhibition.

and more like silver (see Ill. 109). Probably the earliest Britannia metal made in the United States was by Babbitt, Crossman and Company, who were the forerunners of the old New England firm of Reed and Barton. By 1846 Britannia metal was being produced which bore the mark of this latter firm.

Meriden, Connecticut, became one of the great centers for Britannia metal. By 1830 Ashbil Griswold was probably the foremost manufacturer of Britannia in the United States. His wares were sold all over America; it was Griswold who later merged with the Rogers Brothers to found the International Silver Company in Meriden.

The revolutionary discovery was that Britannia metal could be electroplated. The Roger brothers were the first to experiment with this in the 1840's and the new ware came into every American household. Much of it was ill-conceived, with a combination of late eighteenth century shapes and more up-to-date silver shapes dominating. Elaborate engraved ornamentation was often in no manner suited to the piece. In 1855 the catalogue of the Meriden Britannia Company advertised thousands of objects available in this plated metal—104 different patterns of table casters alone were mentioned!

Ironwork. Iron furnaces were among the first essential industries founded in Colonial America. Early iron, however, was fairly limited to necessities and little thought was given to its decorative aspects. By the second quarter of the nineteenth century, the industry had been mechanized to such an extent that iron could now be cast by a complete factory method. This brought about an increased desire for cast household objects. One of the beauties of iron was that the individual parts of a large object could be separately cast; the parts could easily be transported and the whole assembled at the desired place.

Cast iron was used for the production of architectural elements, furniture, fireplace grates, and stoves, as well as smaller decorative objects. Great centers of the industry were in the Albany-Troy area, New York City, and in Philadelphia. The objects were produced in every revival idiom popular during the second half of the century (see Ill. 107). (See also Color Plate B.)

Wrought or hand-fashioned iron continued to be made in more limited quantities throughout the century. This was generally the craft of the local blacksmith. But certain manufacturers, such as W. H. Pries who worked at 33 Canal Street in New York City in the 1830's, combined wrought iron with cast brass and often produced extremely handsome objects (see Ill. 110).

Collector's Notes. Silver has always been a highly desirable collectible because of its intrinsic value. American silver of the seventeenth and eighteenth centuries has been hard to find and has commanded very high prices for a number of years. However, the silver of the early nineteenth century has only recently been of interest to collectors, who have generally concentrated their efforts on earlier objects. Good values are still to be found in this silver. Fine silversmiths can be represented in a collection of spoons from this period. Nineteenth century pewter is quite scarce because it has long been of interest to avid collectors.

While much of the Britannia metal and other plated wares does not appeal esthetically to twentieth century eyes, some investigation can produce objects that are interesting because of their utilitarian value. The buyer must beware of plated pieces that have dents or holes for these are especially difficult to repair because of the low melting point of the material. In most cases, such pieces need to be replated. It is very rare to find the original electroplating intact.

Cast iron objects still exist in great quantities. Those which were used out-of-doors have long been eagerly sought, but smaller household objects can be found. The design is especially important, for some of the objects executed in cast iron were so overdone that the final effect is not rewarding. A sureness of eye and taste is necessary when dealing with objects of this type.

Nineteenth Century Interiors

THIS CHAPTER will present, through a selected group of examples, the style changes that took place in American interiors between 1800 and 1900. In general, the trend is the same as that which has been seen to exist in other categories of furnishings—a change from Classicism at the beginning of the century to eclecticism at its end. The rooms included have been chosen because they illustrate this change; it should be borne in mind that rooms did exist which had more of a mixture of styles.

Classicism was strongly influential in 1800. A room now installed at the Museum of the City of New York (the New York Drawing Room), shows the influence of Adamesque Classicism on interior woodwork and furnishings (see Ill. 111). The woodwork dates c. 1800 and was removed from a house on Greenwich Street. An Adamesque urn and swags decorate the door, which is painted in two contrasting colors, and a classical dentiled molding serves as the cornice. All of the furnishings are in this same spirit—the furniture is by Duncan Phyfe, with the exception of the gaming table, which is by Charles-Honoré Lannuier. Delicacy and balance typify the woodwork and the furnishings.

As has been previously noted, Classical ornament became more archaeologically correct in the 1820's and 1830's under the Empire style. A room from an Albany, New York, house, c. 1835, which is now at The Henry F. du Pont Winterthur Museum (the Empire

Parlor), is an excellent example of an American interior of this type (see Ill. 112). The woodwork is ornamented with anthemion leaves and rosettes and the cornice has an egg-and-dart carved molding. The marble mantelpiece, which is probably Italian, is decorated with a carved panel after Piranesi and is supported by two caryatids. The furniture, all of it of New York origin, is in the heavy archaeological style and in several of the pieces the attempt to reproduce antique forms can be seen. Many of the decorative accessories are French but were made for the American market; however, the table at the far end of the room is set with a Tucker porcelain tea and coffee service.

By the 1840's, books on taste and the decoration of interiors began to deal with the various revival styles that were becoming popular. The Englishman J. C. Loudon published a number of interior views in different styles in his *Encyclopaedia* (1853). One of these was a room so Classical that it resembled the interior of a Greek or Roman temple (Fig. 38), while another was for a library in the Gothic style, complete with a vaulted ceiling (Fig. 39).

Fig. 38 "Grecian" room, from Loudon's *Encyclopaedia* (1853).

Fig. 39 Gothic study, from Loudon's *Encyclopaedia* (1853).

America's own "tastemaker," Andrew J. Downing, also showed a group of interiors in different styles in his *Architecture of Country Houses*. One of the pages shows two parlors, one in the Gothic style and the other in the Norman style (Fig. 40). Still another page illustrates an elaborate library in the Elizabethan style and a sitting room in the bracketed style (Fig. 41). The latter Downing believed to be America's chief original contribution to exterior and interior architecture; in the illustration the brackets may be seen on the walls and ceiling. Still another illustration from Downing shows a far less pretentious room in the Gothic taste (Fig. 42). This room incorporates only the simplest furniture and decorative accessories.

A simplified version of the late Classical and Empire is to be seen in this dining room at "Sunnyside," Washington Irving's home at Tarrytown, New York (see Color Plate H). The woodwork is Classical in inspiration and the furniture, with the exception of the sideboard, is in the late Sheraton tradition. The chairs, however, have the interesting addition of Gothic pointed arches in their backs. The sideboard (shown in Ill. 10) is in the Empire style and has massive lion-paw feet. The porcelains are all French, and the draperies are English silk damask.

Fig. 40 Gothic room (top), and Norman, from Downing's *Country Houses* (1850).

Fig. 41 Elizabethan room (top), and bracketed room, from Downing's *Country Houses* (1850).

By the middle of the century, it was not uncommon to find different revival styles in use in the same house. This is well illustrated by two rooms from the Robert Milligan house built at Saratoga, New York, in 1853. The study and parlor from this house have been installed at The Brooklyn Museum. The study is primarily in the Gothic style, although other exotic influences are to be noted (see Ill. 113). The simple Classical moldings have been used to form the pointed Gothic arch of the niche to the left. The

167

111 "New York Drawing Room," from a house on Greenwich Street, c. 1800. The furniture is by Duncan Phyfe, with the exception of the gaming table, which is by Charles-Honoré Lannuier.

Museum of the City of New York.

112 "Empire Parlor," from a house in Albany, New York, c. 1835. Archaeological Classicism reigns supreme in all of the furnishings of this room.

The Henry Francis du Pont Winterthur Museum.

113 Study, from the house of Robert Milligan, built in Saratoga, New York, in 1853. Elements borrowed from the Gothic, Renaissance, and Saracenic design vocabularies are all mixed here.

The Brooklyn Museum.

114 Moorish room, from the house of John D. Rockefeller, 4 West 54th Street, New York City, c. 1885. An extreme example of the "Turkish Corner," this room was the creation of an interior designer.

The Brooklyn Museum.

115 Dressing room, c. 1870, designed around a mantelpiece taken from the White House. The Renaissance style influences the interior elements and furnishings in this room.

The Brooklyn Museum.

116 Parlor from the Milligan house, Saratoga, New York, 1853. While Rococo is the dominant design influence, Classicism influences the interior architectural detail.

The Brooklyn Museum.

Fig. 42   Simplified Gothic room, from Downing's *Country Houses* (1850).

bookcase is an imposing piece of Gothic furniture; it was made by Henry Bruner of 396 Hudson Street, New York City. The corner cabinet and chairs all have Gothic details, but the desk has carved trophies typical of the Renaissance revival. The drapery treatment is Saracenic in inspiration.

The parlor from the Milligan house further illustrates a mixture of design sources (see Ill. 116). The elaborate molded plaster cornice and ceiling decoration are a combination of Classical and Rococo details. Certainly the marble mantelpiece is Rococo, as is the elaborate gilt mirror over it. The rosewood furniture is in the Louis XV revival style, and was made by Elijah Galusha, of Troy, New York. The draperies and carpet all restate the Rococo with their masses of flowers and scrolls.

"Irving Cliff" was built by Eliphalet Wood at Irvington-on-Hudson, New York, in 1867. The parlor of this house remains much the same as it was when originally furnished (see Color Plate F). Rococo detail is to be seen in the plasterwork and marble man-

170

telpiece. The chandelier has a curious mixture of Classical and Renaissance design. The furniture, which was made in New York in the 1860's, is in the Louis XVI style. A view of a settee from this suite of furniture is shown in Ill. 35. Most of the decorative objects are European, and were acquired as souvenirs of the Grand Tour.

A dressing room of the 1870's has been installed at The Brooklyn Museum (see Ill. 115). The plasterwork detail and fireplace, which is from the White House, have Renaissance elements. The furniture is also in this taste—the dressing table the work of Thomas Brooks & Co. of 127 & 129 Fulton Street, Brooklyn. A completely different concept of an interior of the 1870's is included as the frontispiece of Clarence Cook's *The House Beautiful* (1878) (Fig. 43). This room is dominated by a Georgian feeling, for it was in the late 1870's that Americans began to look to their colonial past and to admire the furnishings of their ancestors. This was the

beginning of the period of reproduced eighteenth century furniture, which has been popular ever since.

A Moorish room, c. 1885, from the house of John D. Rockefeller at 4 West 54th Street in New York City, is now at The Brooklyn Museum (see Ill. 114). The influence of an interior designer is to be seen here, for all of the decorative objects are conceived in the same taste and spirit. This is an elaborate statement of the

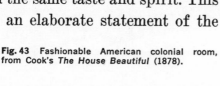
Fig. 43 Fashionable American colonial room, from Cook's *The House Beautiful* (1878).

"Turkish Corner" which was popular in a simplified version throughout the nation. The upholsterer is now more important than the cabinetmaker, for all of the framework of seat furniture is covered over. An armchair from this room is shown in Ill. 44.

Louis C. Tiffany was certainly one of America's most influential interior designers during the late 1880's and 1890's. He decorated the house which Henry O. Havemeyer built at 1 East 66th Street in New York City in 1890. An old photograph survives which shows the extraordinary treatment which Tiffany gave to the stairwell (Fig. 44). The lighting fixtures, in exotic shapes, were

Fig. 44 Stairwell from the H. O. Havemeyer house (1890).

172

made by Tiffany's company, and in cabinets may be seen examples of his glass. The walls were hung with a part of the Havemeyers' famous collection of French Impressionist paintings. The walls are covered in a paper or fabric in a Romanesque pattern which was surely designed by Tiffany. An even more unusual treatment is seen in the studio of Tiffany's own apartment taken from Desmond & Croly's *Stately Homes in America* (1903) (Fig. 45). The fireplace is organic in shape and placed in the center of the room. Moorish lamps, an ostrich egg, and decorative ironwork lend a

Fig. 45 Studio fireplace of L. C. Tiffany's New York apartment, from Desmond & Croly's *Stately Homes* (1903).

bizarre feeling to the room. Tiffany was a collector of Oriental rugs, two of which may be seen in this photograph.

William Henry Vanderbilt began to build a house in New York City in 1879 which stretched for one block (51st to 52nd Street) on Fifth Avenue. The interiors conceived for this house offer an excellent picture of eclecticism at the end of the century. Desmond & Croly's *Stately Homes of America* again shows photographs of these interiors, of which one of the most fantastic is the Japanese room (Fig. 46). Here in a mass of clutter are displayed Oriental objects of every description. The ceiling is vaulted in a Japanese manner, and a material simulating bamboo is used to cover it. Other rooms in the house were conceived in different styles borrowed from divergent sources.

173

Fig. 46 Japanese room of W. H. Vanderbilt's New York house, from Desmond & Croly's *Stately Homes* (1903).

The architectural firm of McKim, Mead, and White was one of America's most influential during the 1890's. Stanford White (1853-1906) was the most famous name associated with this firm; he believed that European taste was far superior to American and the interiors which he decorated prove his convictions. While it is known that he was a furniture designer, and a few documented examples of his work exist, he favored the importation of European antiques—about 1890 or otherwise.

The high priestess of "things European," with a distaste for America's nineteenth century past, was Edith Wharton (1862-1937). With Ogden Codman, Jr., she published *The Decoration of*

174

Houses (1897), in which wealthy Americans were advised how they could create palaces which would rival those of Europe. It is fair to say that, at the dawn of 1900, Americans were looking to Europe for design inspiration and ignoring the achievements of their own nineteenth century.

117 Group of primitive early nineteenth century furnishings used in a bedroom at "Argaty," in North Salem, New York.

Miss Natalie Hays Hammond.

118 Empire and early Victorian furnishings in an apartment building of the late 1920's which overlooks the Hudson River.

Author's collection.

119 Fireplace grouping in the drawing room of a New York City apartment where Louis XV revival furniture, modern paintings, and African sculpture are all in harmony.

Princess Artchil Gourielli.

120 Another view of the drawing room shown in Pl. 119, where more Rococo revival furniture and modern paintings are to be seen.

Princess Artchil Gourielli.

Nineteenth Century Antiques in Modern Settings

THERE IS a bright originality about 19th century antiques which makes them particularly well adapted for use in modern interiors. Unlike the furnishings of the 18th century, most 19th century objects, even when they were conceived in a formal idiom, have a sense of robustness and humor. These objects can give highlights and a new warmth to the most antiseptic modern interior.

The nineteenth century period room does not lend itself to contemporary living. Its well-stuffed, heavily curtained appearance belongs to that century and not to ours. In many instances, individual pieces were lost in the plethora of overelaborate ornament; it is now our task to examine these pieces and to attempt to discover their individual merit.

Edith Wharton and her followers made a decided impression on taste in the early twentieth century with their dislike for American objects and interiors of the nineteenth century. To a large extent, this disregard has persisted until recent years and the period has been derided as one which produced poorly designed mass-produced horrors. For years, 1800 was the terminal date established for many collections; more recently, about 1835 seems to have become more acceptable with the reasoning that it was about this time that the era of the handcraftsman was brought to a close.

However, the influence of mechanization and the use of newly developed materials which ended the era formed the background and springboard for twentieth century design, and a careful look at the objects produced by the new techniques is very rewarding. It does not take long to discover that they are often extremely well designed and executed with great attention to detail. Surely objects from this period should be compatible with contemporary furnishings.

Probably one of the best ways to approach the use of nineteenth century objects in modern interiors is to look at the homes of some individuals who have successfully solved the problem. A sample group of six such houses and apartments has been chosen; in all but one instance, each of the structures was built in the twentieth century. Each presents the owner with a different set of problems and each is solved in a highly personal manner.

Miss Natalie Hays Hammond lives in North Salem, New York, in a house for which she was the architect. The main influence on the first floor at "Argaty," as Miss Hammond calls her house, is formal English Georgian. The owner designed all of the woodwork and interior detail "in the manner of Georgian," as she says. This provides a perfect background for the superb collection of paintings and furniture, mostly of the seventeenth and eighteenth centuries, which the rooms contain. Upstairs, in order to achieve a more informal atmosphere, all interior architectural detail has been omitted, and the woodwork around doors and windows is of the simplest type. On this floor, many of the rooms are decorated with American nineteenth century objects, long one of Miss Hammond's interests. A corner of one of the bedrooms demonstrates what can be done with very few objects (see Ill. 117). The focal point is the primitive pastel portrait of an unknown boy, from New England, c. 1840; the table and Windsor chair are both country pieces—the chair is painted red with gold stenciled decoration, and bears the signature "A. Holmes." A gay New England hooked rug adds a touch of color.

On an entirely different note, Mr. and Mrs. Carl Carmer live in an old house which they call "Octagon House" in Irvington-on-Hudson, New York. Although this extraordinary octagonal edifice was built in the 1860's, their treatment of the interior does not

179

121   Bedroom of a New York City apartment, where innovative nineteenth century furniture is used with modern paintings.

Edgar Kaufmann, jr.

122   Living room of the apartment shown in Plate 121, where innovative nineteenth century furniture is used in a completely modern manner.

Edgar Kaufmann, jr.

123 Living room of a house in Houston, Texas, designed by Philip Johnson. Early Belter side chairs are compatible with a large canvas by Braque and pieces of European furniture.

Mr. and Mrs. John de Menil.

124 The fireplace wall of the same room. A laminated rocking chair near the fireplace seems quite at home with the de Chirico canvases and the settee designed by Charles James.

Mr. and Mrs. John de Menil.

give a museum-room feeling. The shape of the house dictates that some odd geometric rooms would result—the most interesting ones being triangular. In one of these triangular rooms the Carmers house a part of their large collection of wicker furniture, which in summer spills out onto the porch (see Ill. G). These fanciful creations give an almost dream-like feeling when they are combined with blackamoors and other whimsical objects, porcelain figurines and light-hearted paintings. It is obvious that these owners enjoy living with their nineteenth century possessions.

In a small apartment, also along the Hudson River, a slightly earlier feeling pervades the setting (see Ill. 118). The moldings on the wall betray the fact that this apartment building was built during the late 1920's. Empire and Victorian furnishings brighten the background here, for such settings can often be drab. The Empire sofa of the *Récamier* type was possibly made in Philadelphia, and contains the unusual carving of an eagle head and dolphin. To the left stands an armchair by Duncan Phyfe and to the right an elaborate side chair in the manner of the Philadelphian cabinetmaker Antoine G. Quervelle. The tables at either end of the sofa are *papier-mâché,* that at the right bearing the stamped signature "Jennens and Bettridge." The small lacquered table is Chinese export, probably for the American market. French drawings of the early twentieth century are seen reflected in the gilt Empire mirror.

Perfect proof of the adaptability of Victorian antiques to apartment living is shown in the New York City residence of Princess Artchil Gourielli. The enormous drawing room of this apartment, with its oak-paneled walls and elaborate stucco ceiling, is a virtual showcase for modern paintings and the furniture of John Henry Belter. The owner's use of shocking colors in unusual combinations seems to be perfectly in spirit with the Louis XV revival furniture (see Plate G). The paintings are a part of one of the most famous collections in the world, and seen here are the works of such masters as Picasso, Rouault, Vlaminck, and Soutine. The elaboration of carving of the Belter furniture provides a perfect foil for the pictures. Around the fireplace is a grouping of Louis XV revival pieces; the matching sofas are not the work of Belter, but are satisfying in their line (see Ill. 119). Here another interest of the owner reveals itself in African sculpture, again a part of a very famous collection. At the far end of the room, four Belter chairs of different periods are grouped around a circular ottoman (see Ill. 120). A startling but pleasing note is the introduction of the pair of Baroque twisted columns which support full figures of angels. The enormous French vase of blue opaline glass with gilt-bronze mounts is in keeping with the other objects. Surely this room offers evidence that the decorative objects of the nineteenth century can be combined with those of any other period or culture.

Edgar Kaufmann, jr., lives in a New York City apartment where the décor is dominated by the owner's interest in modern design. However, Mr. Kaufmann is equally interested in the forces which have shaped twentieth century design, so it is only natural that he should live with innovative furniture forms of the nineteenth century. In his living room, an iron-braced chair with bundles of coiled springs, of the Turkish frame type, is used with twentieth century classics (see Ill. 122). Another of the owner's interests, Tiffany glass, is to be seen with a large painting of waterlilies by Monet hanging behind the grouping. In the bedroom, a centripetal spring chair by Thomas Warren (patent issued in 1849) provides an interesting contrast to a large painting by Matta which hangs over the bed (see Ill. 121). On the floor beside the bed are a Tiffany Studio lamp of glass and bronze and a nineteenth century spool holder in the shape of a stepped pyramid.

Mr. and Mrs. John deMenil live in Houston, Texas, in a house which was designed by Philip Johnson. The owners' catholic interest in the arts of many eras and cultures is to be seen in every room of the house. The living room offers a view of a lush tropical patio which also serves as a focal point for sculpture (see Ill. 123). Against the far wall hangs a large canvas by Braque. Under it stands a piano which qualifies as a Victorian antique, for it is rosewood Steinway which dates about 1845. On either side of the piano are rosewood Belter side chairs from the early period of that cabinetmaker's career. The settee against the window is Venetian, while the desk in the foreground is Italian provincial. Decorative objects in the room run the gamut from Pre-Columbian to American Indian. The fireplace wall of the deMenil living room is hung with an important group of three paintings by deChirico (see Ill. 124). To the left stands an unusual laminated rosewood rocking chair of the Belter type. The carving of the back reaches such a state of intricacy that one is reminded of lace. The settee was designed by Edward James, and to either side of it are nineteenth century tables with cast iron bases.

There is an unlimited possibility for combining decorative objects of the 19th century with those of other eras. The elaboration of detail of many Victorian furnishings makes them the focal point of contemporary rooms. On the other hand, modern paintings often look well when they are combined with nineteenth century furniture. It is even possible to introduce the nineteenth century into a room which is principally of the eighteenth.

Although there has been a price rise in Victorian antiques in very recent years, it is still possible to find great bargains in small out-of-the-way antique shops. A practical eye and sureness of taste can turn up nineteenth century treasures in unexpected places. These can in turn totally transform a room or a house. It is to be hoped that the reader may in some way be inspired to experiment with the uses of Victorian antiques for himself.

Glossary

Applique—Candle bracket which is affixed to the wall

Ball and spiral twist turning—Lathe turning which resembles a corkscrew with intersecting balls

Baluster leg—Leg with bulbous lathe turning

Beaded molding—Convex rounded molding

Bras de lumière—Arm of a candelabrum

Bright cut—Form of engraving popular circa 1790 in which the metal is removed by beveled cutting, giving a jewel-like faceted sparkle to the surface.

Burled panel—Panel veneered with thin section made from a tree burl

Cabriole leg—Leg whose outline is formed from an elongated cyma curve

Chamfer—Bevel created by cutting away the edge of a piece of wood, stone, etc.

Cartouche—Ornamented tablet or shield sometimes with scrolled elements

Chasing hammer—Tool used in creating relief decoration on the surface of a metallic object

Creamware—White earthenware with a cream-colored glaze

Crocket—Ornament resembling curved foliage which protrudes from a gable, spire, etc.

Diapered pattern—Pattern formed of consistent repeated sections often of a diamond shape

Die cast—Cast from a metal mold

Earthenware—Ceramic vessels made of fired clay, especially the coarser kinds

Egg and dart molding—Ornamental molding composed of oval bosses separated by darts

Etagère—What-not, set of shelves

Feldspar—Crystalline mineral

Finial—Vertical ornament finishing the upper part of a piece of furniture or architecture

Flying shuttle—Mechanical shuttle which could be cast from side to side on the loom

Greek key—Border or pattern composed of lines at right angles to each other

Impressed mark—Mark stamped into ceramic body with a die

Incised mark—Mark cut into ceramic body with a tool

Japanning—Act of coating a surface with a hard, brilliant varnish

Lancet arch—Acutely pointed arch

185

Lustre—Hanging lighting fixture ornamented with drops of cut glass

Nacre—Mother-of-pearl

Ormolu—Brass or bronze gilded to imitate gold

Overglaze—Decoration applied over the glazed surface of a ceramic vessel

Piano lamp—Adjustable floor lamp convenient for reading piano music

Pontil rod—Long iron rod used to hold a glass vessel through the finishing processes

Reeding—A number of semicircular ridges closely arranged in parallel order

Ribbon mark—Stamped or printed mark on a ceramic vessel in a ribbon shape

Shield back—Chair back in shape of heart or classical shield

Slip decorated—Clay applied as raised decoration to a ceramic vessel

Split spindle—Protuberant half spindle applied to a furniture surface

Spool turned—Lathe turning which resembles a group of spools of thread connected together

Stamped mark—Mark printed on a ceramic vessel

Stile—Vertical member of a chair back into which the horizontal is fitted

Stoneware—Earthenware fired at a high temperature

Sulfide—Sulphur compound used in making ornaments set into glass

Swag—Festoon or garland

Thumbpiece—Part of a lid which allows it to be opened with pressure from thumb

Touch mark—Maker's mark applied to metals

Transfer-printing—Process which transfers a printed design to a ceramic surface

Yellow ware—Earthenware with a yellow glaze

Bibliography

Furniture: Books

Albany Institute of History and Art. *New York Furniture Before 1840*. Albany, 1962.

Aslin, Elizabeth. *19th Century English Furniture*. London, 1962.

Biddle, James. *American Art from American Collections*. Loan exhibition: Metropolitan Museum of Art, New York, 1963.

Bjerkoe, Ethel Hall. *The Cabinetmakers of America*. Garden City (N.Y.), 1957.

Bøe, Alf. *From Gothic Revival to Functional Form*. Oslo (Norway), 1957.

Brooklyn Museum. *Victoriana*. Loan exhibition. Brooklyn, 1960.

Chippendale, Thomas. *The Gentleman and Cabinet-Maker's Director*. London, 1762 (third edition).

Cincinnati Cabinet-Maker's Guide Book of Prices. Cincinnati (Ohio), 1827.

Comstock, Helen. *American Furniture*. New York, 1962.

Conner, Robert. *Cabinet Maker's Assistant*. New York, 1842.

The Connoisseur Period Guides. *Early Victorian, 1830-1860*. London, 1958.

————. *Regency, 1810-1830*. London, 1958.

Cook, Clarence. *The House Beautiful*. New York, 1878.

Cornelius, Charles Over. *Furniture Masterpieces of Duncan Phyfe*. New York, 1923.

Downing, Andrew J. *Architecture of Country Houses*. New York, 1850.

————. *Cottage Residences*. New York, 1844.

Eastlake, Charles Locke. *Hints on Household Taste*. London, 1868.

Fildes, George. *Elizabethan Furniture*. London, 1844.

Gibbs-Smith, C. H. *The Great Exhibition of 1851*. London, 1950.

Giedion, Siegfried. *Mechanization Takes Command*. New York, 1948.

Hall, John. *The Cabinet Maker's Assistant*. Baltimore, 1840.

Hamlin, Talbot. *The Greek Revival in America*. New York, 1944.

Hepplewhite, George. *Cabinet-Maker and Upholsterer's Guide*. London, 1788.

Hobhouse, Christopher. *1851 and the Crystal Palace*. London, 1937.

Hope, Thomas. *Household Furniture and Interior Decoration*. London, 1807.

Hughes, Bernard and Therle. *After the Regency*. London, 1952.

Iverson, Marion Day. *The American Chair, 1630-1870*. New York, 1957.

Jones, A. D. *The Illustrated American Biography, ..., Vol. I*. New York, 1852.

Jones, Owen. *Grammar of Ornament*. London, 1856.

Jourdain, Margaret. *Regency Furniture, 1795-1820*. London, 1949.

King, T. *The Modern Style of Cabinet Work*. London, 1832 (second edition).

Lichten, Frances. *Decorative Art of Victoria's Era*. New York, 1950.

BIBLIOGRAPHY

Loudon, J. C. *An Encyclopaedia of Cottage, Farm, and Villa Architecture and Furniture.* London, 1853.

McClelland, Nancy. *Duncan Phyfe and the English Regency, 1795-1830.* New York, 1939.

The Metropolitan Museum of Art. *The Greek Revival in the United States.* Loan exhibition. New York, 1943.

Miller, Edgar G., Jr. *American Antique Furniture.* Vols. 2 and 3. Baltimore, 1937.

The Modern Style of Cabinet Work. London, 1832 (second edition).

Morse, Frances Clary. *Furniture of the Olden Time.* New York, 1902.

Museum of the City of New York. *Furniture by New York Cabinetmakers, 1650-1850.* Loan exhibition, 1956.

Musgrave, Clifford. *Royal Pavilion.* London, 1959.

Nagel, Charles. *American Furniture, 1650-1850.* New York, 1949.

Newark Museum. *Classical America, 1815-1845.* Loan exhibition. Newark (N. J.), 1963.

Nicholson, Peter and Michael Angelo. *The Practical Cabinet Maker, Upholsterer and Complete Decorator.* London, 1826.

Nutting, Wallace. *Furniture Treasury.* Vols. 2 and 3. New York, 1948.

Official Description and Illustrated Catalogue of the Great Exhibition, 1851. 3 vols. London, 1851.

Ormsbee, Thomas H. *Field Guide to American Victorian Furniture.* Boston, 1952.

Percier, Charles, and Pierre F. L. Fontaine. *Recueil de Décorations Intérieures . . .* Paris, 1812.

Pevsner, Nikolaus. *High Victorian Design.* London, 1951.

Pilcher, Donald. *The Regency Style.* London, 1948.

Pugin, A. W. N. *Gothic Furniture in the Style of the Fifteenth Century.* London, 1835.

Randall, Richard H., Jr. *The Furniture of H. H. Richardson.* Loan exhibition: Boston Museum, 1962.

Reade, Brian. *Regency Antiques.* London, 1953.

Roe, F. Gordon. *Victorian Furniture.* London, 1952.

Shaw, Henry. *Specimens of Ancient Furniture.* London, 1836.

Sheraton, Thomas. *The Cabinet-Maker and Upholsterer's Drawing-Book.* London, 1802.

————. *Designs for Household Furniture.* London, 1812.

Sloan, Samuel. *Designs for Rural Buildings.* Philadelphia, 1861.

————. *Sloan's Homestead Architecture.* Philadelphia, 1867.

Smith, George. *The Cabinet-Maker and Upholsterers' Guide.* London, 1826.

————. *A Collection of Designs for Household Furniture and Interior Decoration. . . .* London, 1808.

Smith, Walter. *The Masterpieces of the Centennial International Exhibition.* Vol. II: "Industrial Art." Philadelphia, 1876.

Stephenson, John W. *Furniture Upholstering.* New York, 1914.

The Supplement of the London Chair-Makers'...Book of Prices. London, 1808.

Talbert, Bruce James. *Gothic Forms Applied to Furniture.* London, 1867.

Taylor, M. *Ideas for Rustic Furniture Proper for Garden Seats, Summer Houses, Hermitages, Cottages, etc.* London, 1838.

Wakefield Rattan Company. *Illustrated Catalogue of Rattan and Reed Furniture.* Boston, n.d.

Webster, Thomas. *An Encyclopaedia of Domestic Economy....* London, 1844.

Wheeler, Gervase. *Rural Homes.* New York, 1852.

Whitaker, Henry. *Practical Cabinet-Maker.* London, 1847.

Wyatt, Matthew Digby. *The Industrial Arts of the Nineteenth Century: Illustrations of the Choicest Specimens of the Exhibition of 1851.* London, 1851.

Furniture: Periodicals

Ackermann, Rudolph, ed. *The Repository of Arts, Literature, Commerce, Manufacture, Fashions, and Politics.* London, 1809-1828.

Biddle, James. "Nicholas Biddle's Andalusia, A Nineteenth Century County Seat Today," *Antiques,* September 1964, pp. 286-290.

Butler, Joseph T. "American Mid-Victorian Outdoor Furniture," *Antiques,* June, 1959, pp. 564-567.

————. "Ingenious and Fanciful Victorian Furniture," *Collectors and Collections.* New York, 1961, pp. 113-122.

Cole, Henry. *Journal of Design.* London, 1848-1862.

Cornelius, Charles Over. "The Distinctiveness of Duncan Phyfe," *Antiques,* February, 1922, pp. 205-208.

Davis, Felice. "The Victorians and Their Furniture," *Antiques,* June, 1943, pp. 256-259.

———— "Victorian Cabinetmakers in America," *Antiques,* September, 1943, pp. 111-115.

Downs, Joseph. "The Greek Revival in the United States," *Antiques,* November, 1943, pp. 218-220.

————. "John Henry Belter and Company," *Antiques,* September, 1948, pp. 166-168.

Grand Rapids Furniture Record, April, 1890.

The Horticulturist. "Rustic Furniture—First Article," June, 1858, pp. 304-306.

————. "Rustic Furniture—Second Article," July, 1858, pp. 360-361.

Ingerman, Elizabeth A. "Personal Experiences of an Old New York Cabinetmaker," *Antiques,* November, 1963, pp. 576-580.

Kaufmann, Edgar, jr. "Nineteenth Century Design," *Perspecta,* New Haven (Conn.), n.d.

Melcher, Marguerite F. "Shaker Furniture," *The Philadelphia Museum Bulletin,* Spring, 1962, pp. 89-92.

BIBLIOGRAPHY

Mésangère, Pierre la, ed. *Meubles et Objets de Goût* ....Paris, 1802-1835.

Montgomery, Charles. "John Needles—Baltimore Cabinetmaker," *Antiques,* April, 1954, pp. 292-295.

Otto, Celia Jackson. "The Méridienne," *Antiques,* June, 1963, pp. 675-679.

―――――. "Pillar and Scroll: Greek Revival Furniture of the 1830's," *Antiques,* May, 1962, pp. 504-507.

Pearce, John, Lorraine W. and Smith, Robert C. "The Meeks Family of Cabinetmakers," *Antiques,* April 1964, pp. 414-420.

Pearce, Lorraine Waxman. "American Empire Furniture in the White House," *Antiques,* May, 1962, pp. 516-517.

―――――. "The Lannuier Brothers, Cabinetmakers," *Antiques,* August, 1952, pp. 141-143.

Raley, Robert R. "Interior Designs by Benjamin Henry Latrobe for the President's House," *Antiques,* June 1959, pp. 568-571.

Randall, Richard H., Jr. "Sources of the Empire Style," *Antiques,* April 1963, pp. 452-453.

Ronstrom, Maud O'Bryan. "Seignouret and Mallard, Cabinetmakers," *Antiques,* August 1944, pp. 79-81.

Smith, Robert C. "The Athenaeum's Furniture—1," *Athenaeum Annals,* January 1958, pp. 1-4.

―――――. "The Athenaeum's Furniture—2," *Athenaeum Annals,* September 1958, pp. 1-4.

―――――. "The Classical Style in France and England, 1800-1840," *Antiques,* November 1958, pp. 429-433.

―――――. "Late Classical Furniture in the United States, 1820-1850," *Antiques,* December 1958, pp. 519-523.

―――――. "Gothic and Elizabethan Revival Furniture, 1800-1850," *Antiques,* March 1959, pp. 272-276.

―――――. "Rococo Revival Furniture, 1850-1870," *Antiques,* May 1959, pp. 471-475.

―――――. "Furniture of the Eclectic Decades, 1870-1900," *Antiques,* July 1959, pp. 50-53.

―――――. "'Good Taste' in Nineteenth-Century Furniture," *Antiques,* October 1959, pp. 342-345.

―――――. "Philadelphia Empire Furniture by Antoine Gabriel Quervelle," *Antiques,* September 1964, pp. 304-308.

Ceramics: Books

Barber, Edwin Atlee, *Marks of American Potters.* Philadelphia, 1904.

―――――. *The Pottery and Porcelain of the United States.* New York, 1909.

Barret, Richard Carter. *Bennington Pottery and Porcelain.* New York, 1958.

Cox, Warren. *The Book of Pottery and Porcelain,* Vol. II. New York, 1944.

Madsen, Stephan T. *Sources of Art Nouveau.* New York, 1957.

McKearin, George S. *A Loan Exhibition of Early American Pottery and Early American Glass.* Hoosick Falls (N.Y.), 1931.

Museum of Contemporary Crafts. *Forms from the Earth—1000 Years of Pottery in America.* Loan exhibition, n.d.

Philadelphia Museum of Art. *Tucker China: 1825-1838.* Loan exhibition, 1957.

Prime, William C. *Pottery and Porcelain of All Times and Nations.* New York, 1879.

Ramsay, John. *American Potters and Pottery.* Clinton (Mass.), 1939.

Savage, George. *Porcelain Through the Ages.* London, 1954.

Spargo, John. *Early American Pottery and China.* New York and London, 1926.

Stoudt, A. H. Rice, and John Baer. *The Shenandoah Pottery.* Strasburg (Va.), 1929.

Thorn, C. Jordan. *Handbook of Old Pottery and Porcelain Marks.* New York, 1947.

Watkins, Lura Woodside. *Early New England Potters and Their Wares.* Cambridge (Mass.), 1950.

Ceramics: Periodicals

Barret, Richard Carter. "The Pottery and Porcelain of Bennington," *Antiques,* June 1956, pp. 528-531.

Chandler, R. L. "The Methods of Early American Potters," *Antiques,* April 1924, pp. 174-178.

Graham, John Meredith, II. "Ceramics Used in America," *American Collector,* October 1947, pp. 30-32.

Koch, Robert. "Rookwood Pottery," *Antiques,* March 1960, pp. 288-289.

Ramsay, John. "Early American Pottery: A Résumé," *Antiques,* October 1931, pp. 224-229.

Schwartz, Marvin D. "A Gift of Early American Ceramics," *Brooklyn Museum Bulletin,* Winter 1956, pp. 1-2.

———. "Fine American Ceramics of the Victorian Period," *Antiques,* April 1960, pp. 386-389.

Watkins, Lura Woodside. "Henderson of Jersey City and His Pitchers," *Antiques,* December 1946, pp. 389-392.

Glass: Books

Belknap, E. M. *Milk Glass.* New York, 1940.

Bergstrom, E. H. *Old Glass Paperweights.* Chicago, 1940.

Chipman, F. W. *The Romance of Old Sandwich Glass.* Sandwich (Mass.), 1932.

Knittle, Rhea Mansfield. *Early American Glass.* New York and London, 1927.

Lee, Ruth Webb. *Early American Pressed Glass.* Northborough (Mass.), 1931.

———. *Sandwich Glass.* Northborough (Mass.), 1939.

———. *Victorian Glass.* Northborough (Mass.), 1944.

McClinton, Katharine Morrison. *American Glass.* Cleveland (Ohio), 1950.

McKearin, George S. and Helen. *American Glass.* New York, 1941.

BIBLIOGRAPHY

—————. *Two Hundred Years of American Blown Glass.* New York, 1950.

Museum of Contemporary Crafts. *Louis Comfort Tiffany.* Loan exhibition: New York, 1958.

Rose, James H. *The Story of American Pressed Glass of the Lacy Period, 1825-1850.* New York, 1954.

Watkins, Lura Woodside. *American Glass and Glassmaking.* New York, 1950.

—————. *Cambridge Glass,* 1818-1888. Boston, 1931.

Wilson, Kenneth M. *Glass in New England.* Sturbridge (Mass.), 1959.

Glass: Periodicals

Bradshaw, W. R. "Favrile Glass," *The House Beautiful,* March 1900, pp. 275-279.

Davidson, Marshall B. "Similarity of Ancient and American Glass," *American Collector,* August 1942, pp. 14-17.

Feld, Stuart B. "Nature in Her Most Seductive Aspects: Louis Comfort Tiffany's Favrile Glass," *Metropolitan Museum Bulletin,* November 1962, pp. 101-112.

Innes, Lowell. "Pittsburgh White and Clear and the Bakewell Patent," *Antiques,* June 1961, pp. 557-559.

Kaufmann, Edgar, jr. "Tiffany, Then and Now," *Interiors,* February 1955, pp. 82-86.

Lee, Ruth Webb. "The Duncan Trio," *Antiques,* April 1933, pp. 132-134.

—————. "Pittsburgh versus Sandwich," *Antiques,* June 1956, pp. 526-527.

Rose, James H. "Wheeling Lacy Glass," *Antiques,* June 1956, pp. 526-527.

Watkins, Lura Woodside. "Deming Jarvis and the Pressing of Glass," *Antiques,* October 1931, pp. 218-220.

Lighting Devices: Books

Earle, Alice Morse. *Homelife in Colonial Days.* New York, 1898.

Hayward, Arthur H. *Colonial Lighting.* New York, 1962.

Hough, Walter. *Collection of Heating and Lighting Utensils in the United States National Museum.* Washington (D.C.), 1928.

Mercer, Henry C. *Light and Fire Making.* Doylestown (Pa.), 1898.

Sears and Roebuck Company. *Catalogue.* Chicago, 1900.

Thwing, Leroy. *Flickering Flames.* Rutland (Vt.), 1958.

Watkins, C. Malcolm. *Artificial Lighting in America, 1830-1860.* Washington (D.C.), 1952.

Lighting Devices: Periodicals

Franklin Institute Journal, 1830 and 1834.

Gillingham, Harold E. "An Historic Lamp," *Antiques,* April 1928, pp. 293-294.

Hayward, Arthur H. "Patented Lamps of the Last Century," *Antiques,* February 1934, pp. 49-51.

Watkins, C. Malcolm. "A Lamp Dealer Illustrates His Wares," *Antiques*, June 1939, pp. 297-299.

————. "The Collections: Lighting Devices," *Antiques*, September 1955, pp. 244-247.

————. "Electric Light in Antique Settings," *Antiques*, December 1947, pp. 432-435.

————. "The Whale-Oil Burner: Its Invention and Development," *Antiques*, April 1935, pp. 148-149.

Watkins, Lura Woodside. "Development of Gas Lighting," *Rushlight*, 1943, pp. 5-8.

Wyant, Major L. B. "The Etiquette of Nineteenth-Century Lamps," *Antiques*, September 1936, pp. 113-117.

Silver and Metalwork: Books

Art Institute of Chicago. *Dinner with the Presidents*. Loan exhibition, 1961.

Brix, M. *List of Philadelphia Silversmiths and Allied Artificers from 1682-1850*. Philadelphia, 1920.

Buhler, Kathryn C. *American Silver*. Cleveland, 1950.

Currier, Ernest M. *Marks of Early American Silversmiths*. Portland (Me.), 1938.

Ensko, Stephen G. C. *American Silversmiths and Their Marks*, New York, 1927-1948.

Fales, Martha Gandy. *American Silver in the Henry Francis du Pont Winterthur Museum*, Winterthur (Del.), 1958.

French, Hollis. *A List of Early American Silversmiths and Their Marks*, New York, 1917.

Groce, George, and David H. Wallace. *New York Historical Society Dictionary of Arts in America*. New Haven (Conn.), 1957.

Kauffman, Henry J. *Early American Copper, Tin, and Brass*. New York, 1950.

Laughlin, Ledlie Irwin. *Pewter in America*. 2 volumes. New York, 1940.

Lindsay, J. Seymour. *Iron and Brass Implements of the English and American Home*. Boston and London, n.d.

Maryland Historical Society. *Silver by Maryland Craftsmen, 1721-1880*. Loan exhibition, 1953.

Mercer, Henry Chapman. *The Bible in Iron*. Doylestown (Pa.), 1914.

Phillips, John Marshall. *American Silver*. New York, 1949.

Rice, Norman S. *Albany Silver 1652-1825*. Albany (N.Y.), 1964.

Swank, James M. *History of the Manufacture of Iron in All Ages and Particularly in the United States from Colonial Times to 1891*. Philadelphia, 1892.

Taylor, Gerald. *Silver*. London, 1956.

Thorn, C. Jordan. *Handbook of American Silver and Pewter Marks*. New York, 1949.

Virginia Museum of Fine Arts. *Masterpieces of American Silver*. Loan exhibition, 1960.

BIBLIOGRAPHY

Wenham, Edward. *The Practical Book of American Silver*. Philadelphia and New York, 1949.

Wyler, S. B. *The Book of Old Silver, English, American, Foreign*. New York, 1937.

Silver and Metalwork: Periodicals

Fales, Martha Gandy. "English Design Sources of American Silver," *Antiques*, January 1963, pp. 82-85.

Holloway, H. Maxson. "History in American Silver," *American Collector*, November 1946, pp. 10-12.

King, Pauline. "A Collection of Copper and Brass," *The House Beautiful*, January 1900, pp. 67-71.

Phillips, John Marshall. "Silver in the World of Washington Irving," *American Collector*, October 1947, pp. 22-24.

Textiles: Books

Bowles, Ella Shannon. *Homespun Handicrafts*. Philadelphia, 1931.

Brockett, L. P. *The Silk Industry in America*. New York, 1876.

Couzot, Henri, and Frances Morris. *Painted and Printed Fabrics*. New York, 1927.

Cummings, Abbott Lowell. *Bed Hangings*. Boston, 1961.

Fennelly, Catherine. *Textiles in New England, 1790-1840*. Sturbridge (Mass.), 1961.

Finley, Ruth E. *Old Patchwork Quilts*. Philadelphia, 1929.

Harbeson, Georgiana Brown. *American Needlework*. New York, 1938.

Kenrick, William. *The American Silk Grower's Guide*. Boston, 1837.

Little, Frances. *Early American Textiles*. New York, 1931.

Peto, Florence. *American Quilts and Coverlets*. New York, 1949.

Tilton, John Kent. *Two Hundred Years of Textile Design*. New York, n.d.

Vanderpoel, Emily Noyes. *American Lace and Lace-Makers*. New Haven (Conn.), 1924.

Whiting, Gertrude. *Tools and Toys of Stitchery*. New York, 1928.

Textiles: Periodicals

Born, W. "Early American Textiles," *Ciba Review*, October 1949, pp. 27-87.

Clark, Raymond B. "Historical Handkerchiefs," *New York State History*, April 1955, pp. 189-196.

Mailey, Jean. "Printed Textiles in America," *Antiques*, May 1956, pp. 422-427.

Peacock, Florence. "Samplers," *The House Beautiful*, March 1900, pp. 262-268.

White, Margaret E. "Printed Textiles of Europe and America," *The Museum*, Winter 1960, pp. 18-23.

Nineteenth Century Interiors: Books

Andrews, Wayne. *Architecture Ambition and Americans*. New York, 1955.

Desmond, Harry W., and Herbert Croly. *Stately Homes in America*. New York, 1903.

Gloag, John. *Victorian Taste*. New York, 1962.

Halsey, R. T. H. and Elizabeth Tower. *The Homes of Our Ancestors*. Garden City (N.Y.), 1935.

Kettell, Russell Hawes (ed.). *Early American Rooms, 1650-1858*. Portland (Me.), 1936.

Pratt, Richard. *Treasury of Early American Homes*. New York, 1949.

Praz, Mario. *An Illustrated History of Furnishing*. New York, 1964.

Rogers, Meyric R. *American Interior Design*. New York, 1947.

Scully, Vincent J., Jr. *The Shingle Style*. New Haven (Conn.), 1955.

Wharton, Edith, and Ogden Codman, Jr. *The Decoration of Houses*. New York, 1902.

Winchester, Alice (ed.). *Living with Antiques*. New York, 1963.

Nineteenth Century Interiors: Periodicals

Andrews, Wayne. "A Gothic Tragedy in Bridgeport?" *Antiques*, July 1957, pp. 50-53.

Belting, Natalia Maree. "Mid-Victorian," *Antiques*, September 1949, pp. 169-171.

Butler, Joseph T. "A Case Study in Nineteenth-Century Color: Redecoration at Sunnyside," *Antiques*, July 1960, pp. 54-56.

_____. "A Hudson River Valley Portfolio," *Antiques*, April 1964, pp. 432-437.

_____. "Two Documented Nineteenth Century Rooms," *Antiques*, June 1958, pp. 551-553.

Kaufmann, Edgar, jr. "At Home with Louis C. Tiffany," *Interiors*, December 1957, pp. 116-124.

Kimball, Fiske. "Victorian Art and Victorian Taste," *Antiques*, March 1933, pp. 103-105.

Little, Nina Fletcher. "The General Salem Towne House at Old Sturbridge Village," *Antiques*, April 1959, pp. 358-365.

McLanathan, Richard B. K. "History in Houses: Fountain Elms in Utica, New York," *Antiques*, April 1961, pp. 356-363.

Nagel, Charles. "Four Nineteenth-Century Interiors," *Antiques*, December 1953, pp. 470-472.

Ralston, Ruth. "Nineteenth-Century New York Interiors," *Antiques*, June 1943, pp. 266-270.

Wilson, Samuel, Jr. "The Pontalba 1850 House," *Antiques*, July 1956, pp. 58-59.

Index

Page numbers in *italics* refer to illustrations.

INDEX

INDEX

INDEX

202